THE GOD I BELIEVE IN AND WHY

Maurice Reidy

The God I Believe In
and Why

the columba press

First published in 2006 by
the columba press
55A Spruce Avenue, Stillorgan Industrial Park,
Blackrock, Co Dublin

Cover by Bill Bolger
Origination by The Columba Press
Printed in Ireland by ColourBooks Ltd, Dublin

ISBN 1 85607 533 8

Acknowledgements
Scripture quotations are taken from the Jerusalem Bible Version Bible,
copyright (c) 1966, 1967 and 1968 by Darton, Longman and Todd Ltd
and Doubleday and Company Inc., and are used by permission.

Table of Contents

We ourselves have known and put our faith in God's love towards ourselves. God is love and anyone who lives in love lives in God, and God lives in him. (1 John 4:16)

You did not see him, yet you love him; and still without seeing him, you are already filled with a joy so glorious that it cannot be described, because you believe; and you are sure of the end to which your faith looks forward, that is, the salvation of your souls. (1 Peter 1:8-9)

See, *(verb)*. Have or use the power of perceiving with the eye; descry, discern by sight, observe, look at ...; discern mentally, attain to comprehension of, ascertain by search or inquiry or reflection ... etc., etc. see *The Pocket Oxford Dictionary*, 1942 (Fourth Edition), Oxford.

Introduction

We live in an age that finds it increasingly difficult, if not impossible, to believe in God. It seems that to many of us the very notion of a supreme being who belongs outside of the universe, as well as within it, is one that is beyond any form of comprehension. Add to this the idea of an invitation from God to men and women to love him because he has first loved us (I use the personal pronoun conscious of its limitations with regard to gender), and to spend eternity in complete happiness in his company, and you have the reason why so many simply throw up their hands at what appears to be the fantasy of it all.

Our age would have us believe, nonetheless, in the wonders of human technology and science. It would want us to delete from our minds whatever might conflict with what can be sensed and measured, and to take our stand only on such material planning as will lead to human happiness. Yet saying it as simply as this indicates the impossibility of such a project. For each of us, being a human person means so much more than the fulfilment of the senses and the mere measurement of things. On this basis only the 'human' aspect of each person is going to be meaningless.

There are many works that explore in varying degrees of detail what it is that Christians believe. This book looks more closely at the actual change that takes place when a person moves from asking about the existence of God to making an act of faith in God. That is the move that I wish to explore. In studying that move, I want to show how it is that religious knowledge and belief are valid. The book situates itself in that space where things are justified, where matters of faith are shown to have meaning, or where the context in which belief makes sense is explained.

It is impossible to approach religious faith without some sense of the purpose or meaning of human creation. As we know, many people today imagine that humanity has no meaning whatsoever; save whatever meanings we human beings may wish to bring to it. In this book, I want to show that some kind of outside perspective, one that is not totally subjective, is always both possible and likely.

With regard to my own thinking, I am a believer. While I have given much thought to various forms of unbelief, I do not subscribe to them. Yet, unbelief has frequently appeared to me to be a more attractive option. My own temptations to religious unbelief have always centred on the whole issue of God, that is, whether there is anything at all that exists beyond that which can be perceived with the senses. In this sense I can say that I am a person of one great doubt rather than of a host of lesser ones. I think it is this structure of thought that leads me to make an argument that attempts to show the 'whole picture' of God. This is my argument. For me, because God plainly exists, lesser difficulties tend to diminish in importance. In this overall perspective, it seems that God is 'there', that the Judeo-Christian tradition has reflected God's presence in the world for some four thousand years, and that the darkness and the difficulties that undeniably exist are ultimately illuminated by God's 'invisible' light, if I may put it that way.

What I have tried to set out here are the grounds for faith as understood in the Catholic faith. My hope is that these pages may be of help to ordinary Catholics in understanding their own belief. And I would like to think that they would be of interest also to readers of other faiths or of none. Inevitably, in this process, I fall back on the use of some terms and phrases that have become part of the language of Christianity. To the best of my ability, I have attempted to explain the meaning of such terms to readers who may be unfamiliar with them.

The book can be seen as an exploration of two related ideas, faith and knowledge. Faith is the perception of that which cannot be seen; what the believer perceives is taken on a judgement of trust. Knowledge, on the other hand, is a 'coming to terms' with facts as revealed by our perception of them. But knowledge depends on human judgement, as does faith, and yet our judgement can be false. I have tried to bring together in the context of

our fallible judgements and of our scientific age these two intellectual realities of faith and knowledge.

It will be noticed that I frequently include reference to when
an author lived. I feel that this inclusion helps to create a greater
sense of awareness concerning the time scale involved in the
growth and development of religion. It comes naturally to me to
draw on the work of John Henry Newman (1801-1890) as I have
had the opportunity to study his thought at close quarters. To
me, his theory of knowledge is readily accessible and makes
clear sense.

The book could not have been written without the help of
many people. It can be a difficult and daunting task to talk about
one's intimate thoughts on religious matters in the presence of
another person and a tape recorder. I would like to thank very
sincerely the four people who undertook that task and gave me
extended interviews on their own understandings of religious
knowledge and belief. In my text they are named simply as
Suzanne, Paula, Declan and Martin. These are not their real
names. Their views, each of them different in style and in concern, including one that professes to no Christian belief at all,
have been immensely helpful to me in bringing out different aspects of the theme of faith. They contribute to the book a real
sense of the immediacy of ordinary experience – lived lives of
belief and unbelief. They have sharpened my argument, and
provide contrasts with aspects of it.

My sincere thanks are due also to Rev John Jones, parish
priest of Blanchardstown, for his constant encouragement over
many years, and to Joseph Dunne of St Patrick's College,
Drumcondra, who made many valuable comments and sugges-
tions on the chapters that relate to philosophy.

In particular, I would like to thank Dorothy and William
Scally who have ploughed through many drafts of the different
chapters. Their incisive comments have always been supportive
and encouraging. Without their patience, guidance and support,
there would be no book. The faults that remain are my own.

CHAPTER ONE

The Faith of the Ordinary Person

Religious faith is a willingness to trust in God, a willingness to trust that God exists and is near, whatever the appearances to the contrary may indicate. The words 'faith' and 'trust' stem from much the same idea, the one being almost a synonym for the other. Yet once the word 'trust' is introduced, the reality that is spoken of seems at once to become more personal, more a matter between two people who understand each other. This touches upon the essence of what is meant by religious faith.

The act of faith is an ordinary act of assent. This assent, saying 'yes', is to the presence of God and to the reality of our being in communication with him. It is like many other acts of saying 'yes' that are for the most part taken for granted by those who make them. It is an assent to what is perceived to be real. The act of faith is like the act of listening to a melody or a piece of music as opposed to analysing it closely or criticising it. Such acts of assent turn upon that which is understood to be real, that impresses with its sense of reality. The assent of faith links the believer directly to God: the principal reality that is at the heart of Christian faith is the reality of encountering God.

For the Christian, the term 'ordinary believer' is used in the sense of 'everyman' or of each person. It does not presuppose any special training or expertise. It presumes that God calls everybody to a life of faith, although not everybody actually subscribes to belief. There are many who believe in ordinary and unremarkable ways who are scarcely aware of this fact. The Christian religion provides a home for all ordinary believers.

Suzanne, although she no longer describes herself as a believer, gave this account of the faith of her mother:

My mother lost her own mother when she was born, and her life, all her life, she has looked forward to meeting her mother, and she firmly believes she will meet the person who is her mother when she dies. I envy that kind of faith. I don't have that kind of faith, and yet I don't know what ... like everybody, I don't know what happens. What happens when you die is the great question ...

This idea of Suzanne's mother looking forward to meeting her own mother, whom she had never actually met in this life, but of whom she had heard, is an example of how, for many believers, God is simply accepted and understood as being there. The act of believing is not primarily concerned with ideas about God, or with religious doctrines, but with God himself, as he is. It ends not in statements about God, but in God.[1] The act of faith turns upon direct contact with God.

Because the reality of God is something that is infinitely superior to the human mind, we ought not to be surprised that an act that reaches into God should be largely insensible on our part. We are not talking about sense knowledge, about what can be seen, touched, heard, observed. Faith is not about sense knowledge, it is about 'things not seen and not heard'.[2] The interplay of trust and confidence that takes place between the person and God takes place without sight and without sound. We read in St Paul that 'The word is near you, on your lips and in your heart (that is, the word of faith which we preach)'.[3] This 'word' is a largely silent word.

In faith, one person comes into real contact with another, yet that contact is one that is subject to a prior trust and belief in what has been told. The act of faith is not unlike a blind man running his hand over the face of his own child. The blind man

---

1. See St. Thomas Aquinas (1224-1274): *Summa Theologica*, 2-2, q. 1, art. 2, ad secundum.

2. 1 Cor 1:9

3. Rom 10:6-8. Paul is here quoting a text already some thousand years old from the teaching of Moses in the book of Deuteronomy 30:14: 'but the word is very near you; it is in your mouth and in your heart, so that you can do it.'

knows his own child because he has always been given to understand that this child was his.

Faith in God comes before knowing very much about God.
One begins to realise that there is 'something' or 'someone' there
beyond the appearances of the world. An awareness that God *is*
follows upon this realisation. The immediate experience is one
of God simply being there. It is like the comparison with a
melody, or the child.

Believing is not primarily concerned with a conceptual account
of God then, with ideas about God or with religious doctrines as
such. In this sense, believing is to be distinguished from study,
even from studying the things that have to do with God, which
is the province of theology. Theology, of its nature, tends to be
notional, speculative and abstract in its approach, whereas faith
is concrete, it is 'now'. Faith is actual, it is alive and it is real; it is
an experience that somehow or other engages the whole person.
God cannot be understood by intellect alone.[4]

A few simple words, and the implications that follow from
them, convey much that is to be known about God. 'One',
'three', 'person', 'God', 'Father', 'Son', 'Spirit': these few words
lead us on eventually to all that we can know conceptually about
the nature of God. They are not specialised or technical words,
nor are they in any way 'scientific' words. They are common
words. In the New Testament and the literature of the early
church we are introduced to them. It is when we combine them
and attempt to analyse their meaning, which is a most reasonable thing to do, that we run into what we call 'mystery'.[5]

Christians believe that in Jesus Christ they possess the full
revelation, insofar as the human person is capable of receiving it,
of what God is. This 'incarnation' perspective of God allows all
of those personal details of God to be sketched in, details that
would not be known otherwise. In the New Testament we have,

4. St Thomas Aquinas asserts that the existence of God is not self-evid-
ent to the human mind. *Op. cit.*, 1a, 2, 1, sed contra.
5. J. H. Newman, *A Grammar of Assent* (1870), New York (Image Books
Edition) 1955, page 113. My paragraph attempts to summarise
Newman on these points.

as it were, a perfect human image of what the personality of God is like, because Jesus is, in a very special sense, God.

Faith and prayer are closely linked. This is because the act of faith takes place at the core of our being, at a level where we recognise that the most important decisions of all are taken, the level we call our soul. Prayer is the speech of the soul. This immediacy of faith to prayer and to the core of our being emerges from my conversation with Martin:

Eventually it came to a stage when I couldn't pray, I don't know at what stage that occurred. I couldn't say formal prayers so I gave them up completely, and I went in and I said my own prayers. I said 'I'm here … You're there. Will you just listen to me for a few minutes?' And I came on my own terms. They say you shouldn't be making your own terms, but I think that it's necessary to make your own terms and to maintain your individuality …

We have here a certain maturity and a person taking responsibility for his own speech with God. He arrives at a place where learned forms of prayer are no longer possible for him, and so he enters on his own personal dialogue with his creator. And so, in responding to Jesus, it is much more natural and possible for us to respond to God in the way we would respond to a perfect and wonderful person. This is simply what happens by virtue of our belief in the incarnation of God. When we pray to Jesus, we are praying to God. These themes also emerge in a very characteristic way from my conversation with Paula. I asked her where was God in her life:

He's there. I am a strong believer that he is there. And I pray; I get the kids to pray, I bring the kids to Mass. Anything happens, the first person I call on is 'Himself'.

As the conversation continued, Paula's impressions of God took on a more personal and intimate character:

Like a counsellor up there … I mean, better talking to someone than talking on your own and answering yourself back … Yes, as a counsellor … To be honest, I never actually thought … until you were actually speaking to me … I never thought I actually had these

*feelings. Somebody there that you could actually share everything
with. Like having another husband as such, but a counsellor, a boss,
that you can tell them absolutely everything, and no matter what
happens, at the end of the day, well so they say in the Bible, he'll forgive you. As long as you ask for forgiveness, he'll forgive you.*

I put it to her that she never felt that she was on her own…
*Exactly, exactly, exactly … I mean I never actually thought I had
these … I never thought so deep … I mean I would say I'm a
Christian, I am a good Christian … do my bit … have my bad side
as well, like everybody else … but I never actually thought, until
you started talking, that I actually felt as deeply as I do. Its not
until you are asked, I suppose, that you realise how deep your religion actually is. I feel really, really sad for people that don't have
anything …*

Then the conversation took a sudden and strange turn. Paula
said:
He has his moments … then so do most men (laughing) …

You think of God as a man?
*Yes. Very much so … I keep saying … as in women, as in the things
women have to go through … being a woman, having a baby, having
a period, going through the menopause … I keep saying: 'It's easy
knowing God was a man …' I always say that, always … that's one
thing he'll get me for when I get up there, because I always say that,
'easy knowing he was a man.' He didn't make life easy for a woman,
even though his mother was a woman, you know … definitely a
man, definitely, definitely a man (laughing).*

Here we were stumbling on the real faith perspectives of one
young Dublin woman, rooted very much in her own perceptions of herself and her experience. With Paula, it was not possible to discuss these matters in an abstract or distant tone; she
was not familiar with arguments nor with the more exact definitions of theology. Her approach to the whole question of God
was particular and it was concrete. When she thought of God
she thought immediately of him as incarnate in Jesus, although
it took me a moment to recognise this. Yet she was very certain

that she had direct knowledge of God. And when she thought of
Mary, the mother of Jesus, she identified spontaneously with
her as a woman and as a mother. There is no suggestion on
Paula's part of a flight into some sacred myth regarding her.

When we are told that Mary the mother of Jesus prayed: 'My
soul glorifies the Lord, my spirit rejoices in God my saviour',[6]
we recognise an outpouring of gratitude to God that is deeply
characteristic of faith. In Mary's case, as we would expect, her
faith was profoundly informed by her knowledge of God drawn
from her own Jewish religion. The word 'prayer' is almost another synonym for the word 'faith'.

Although the act of faith of each person ends in God, individual impressions of God can vary greatly. It is completely understandable that each of us would have a personal impression of
the infinite God, especially when we realise that our impressions
of finite things can be personal and individual. There is nothing
at all unique to Paula in this. We see the same thing every day in
people's own impressions of their parents, and indeed in their
impressions of their own place in society or of how they are held
by their friends.

So religious faith is an understanding of God that is direct
and immediate. The possession of faith puts people in touch
with the reality of God, although it does not guarantee that a
person's impressions of God are always correctly expressed. By
this I mean simply that the prayer of Jesus, for example, the 'Our
Father', expresses perfectly what he knew of the Father. Our impressions, on the contrary, are tied in for better and for worse
with our own understandings of fatherhood, including of course
our understanding of the fatherhood of God. When we reflect on
it, religious faith is very normal in the world. Ordinary people
have faith and they exercise it all the time.

Religious darkness
Faith can be a blank kind of knowledge. A quality of seeming
emptiness sometimes permeates it. In other words, the light that

6. Lk 1:46-47.

accompanies certainty about God disappears, or never appears. It can happen that we are left with a vague sense of nothingness, a sense of 'so what'. For many believers there can be a leave-taking of the 'comfort' knowledge of faith. This is a common experience. Yet the darkness that follows faith is very different from the darkness that occurs before faith is discovered. Something like this can happen when we have been exposed to great suffering.

Part of the problem of religious darkness is the enormity of the concept of God and the ordinary routine of day-to-day life, as we know it. Life in the ordinary world offers what seems a 'mismatch' to eternity, where there is life unending in another world. Inevitably, we are always close-wrapped in our own human culture and our own perception of that other world. It is difficult to sustain any kind of appreciative awareness over time of what is involved in having been created or redeemed by God. All believers speak of ebb and flow in their experience of faith. Frequently, after enthusiasm at the beginning, the consolation of God's presence is caught more in a moment off guard, in a word of kindness shared with somebody, in the sunlight appearing after the rain.

The darkness of ordinary faith is illustrated very well in texts that come down to us from ancient times. Obvious examples are some of the psalms of the Old Testament. These songs in praise of God were written down many centuries before the coming of Christ. They reveal very well the personal territory of belief. Time and time again the psalmist cries out to God to show himself; yet he never cries out in disbelief.

In psalm 43 we read at the beginning:
We heard with our ears, O God,
our fathers have told us the story
of the things you did in their days,
you yourself, in days long ago.

Towards the middle we read:
Yet now you have rejected us, disgraced us:
you no longer go forth with our armies.

You make us retreat from the foe
and our enemies plunder us at will.
You make us like sheep for the slaughter,
and scatter us among the nations.

And in the last stanza we read:
Awake, O Lord, why do you sleep?
Arise, do not reject us for ever!
Why do you hide your face from us
And forget our oppression and misery?
For we are brought down low to the dust;
Our body lies prostrate on the earth.
Stand up and come to our help!
Redeem us because of your love!

It can happen that we can read these words and yet not hear or understand what is being said. It is as if the 'religious language' somehow goes over our heads. The words are a cry to a God who does not appear to be listening. They remind us powerfully that the reality of belief has not changed that greatly over the last three thousand years. They remind us also that this difficult and stubborn aspect of faith is the very faith that is endorsed in God's revelation to us.

When we turn to psalm 76, this is what we read:
I cry aloud to God,
Cry aloud to God that he may hear me.

In the day of my distress I sought the Lord.
My hands were raised at night without ceasing;
My soul refused to be consoled.
I remembered my God and I groaned.
I pondered and my spirit fainted ...

I said: 'This is what causes my grief;
That the way of the Most High has changed.'
I remember the deeds of the Lord,
I remember your wonders of old ...

The opening lines of Psalm 42 are frequently quoted for their lyrical quality:

As the deer longs for running streams,
so longs my soul for thee, O God.
My soul thirsts for God, for the living God.

Yet the lines that follow that opening, still in the first stanza of the psalm, are less familiar to many:

When shall I come and behold the face of God?
My tears have been my food day and night,
While men say to me continually, 'Where is your God?'

All of the prayer that is the remainder of psalm 42 takes place in an atmosphere of utter darkness. If the act of faith takes place frequently in darkness, it is no less true that the texts of revelation are framed in an atmosphere that is totally human and recognisable. The perception of the God of Christianity, and of Judaism, is a perception that resonates with us when the questioning of the heart is most genuine and most desperate. The evidence shows that some of our own deepest questions have been lived by many who have gone before us in faith.

These texts, and many more from throughout the psalms, and from other parts of the scriptures, communicate to us a basic truth about belief. It is that truth that we meet in the request spoken to Jesus in the gospel: 'I believe; help my unbelief!'[7] Many believing people live out their lives, or large portions of their lives, in what can only be called religious darkness. To the outside observer looking in at such people, it appears more 'as if' there were a loving God rather than that 'there is' such. Pressed for a further explanation of this, they may put it in some way like Martin. I had begun by saying that we live at a time when religion is treated as if it were simply a quality of a former age without relevance to this one; that many of our friends are not religious in any sense that is obvious to them or to us.

I often wonder whether it is a passing phase ... You see families
where the father and the mother are deeply religious, regular atten-

---

7. Mk 9:24

ders at Mass and prayers and so on, and where the children seem to lose all interest in matters of religion. There is so little to remind one of 'the other world'. This is the trouble ... God himself doesn't help ... in fact he makes it extremely difficult. I don't know whether it is because of his sense of humour or what, but he seems to enjoy ... I won't say he seems to enjoy it but he certainly doesn't do anything to stop an immense aridity in people who do believe and who would like to have a stronger faith, but who go through years of total dryness ...

Here we find an absolute confidence in God accompanied by bewilderment at the experience of a life that has been led largely with a sense of God's absence. I asked whether Martin ever questioned the existence of God:

That is my constant; I don't say occasionally, it is constant. I mean for the last ten, twenty, years now, I've gone through total aridity. I feel like the prior in Brian Moore's lovely novel in a remote monastery somewhere in West Cork. He's lost totally his belief in God, and he leads his monks into prayers, into various ceremonies, and the only prayer that remains to him is the Our Father, and he begins the Our Father, or at least he leads his confreres into the Our Father, but he can't finish it. Now the only prayer that I have been able to say for years is the Our Father. Except the prayer to the Holy Spirit, 'Come Holy Spirit, fill the hearts of your faithful and enkindle in them the fire of your divine love ...' I constantly say that, why I don't know, but I feel the need to say it.

What keeps you going in all this aridity?

Because I know, you see. Even when I don't believe I know, it's one of those strange things; I know that I know. It's like the disciples said to Christ, when he said to them: 'Are you also going to go away?' And they said to him 'Where will we go?' Not because they didn't want to go, but because they had nowhere else to go. I'm in the same boat: I've nowhere else to go. And if I were to throw all that I have lived by over the past seventy years aside, I'd certainly have nowhere to go. So I'm not just hanging on because of that, but because, as I say, I have to believe that what he said is true and that he does fulfil his promises.

Once again, as was the case with Paula, we are in deeply subjective, that is, personal, territory, although here it is not anything like the consolation that she experienced. 'Aridity', which
is so familiar to Martin, can present itself in different forms.
People can experience something like this in their own awareness of themselves, a sense of deep unease, a sense of depres-
sion. Those who have been unfortunate in their lives or in their
life choices can also experience a sense of having been forgotten
by God. This in turn leads them to question whether God really
exists. The important point to bear in mind is that faith can co-
exist with any of these mental states. Faith does not promise
happiness now, although very often it does bring with it happiness and peace.

The very faithfulness of such people to what they believe,
their goodness in every respect and their disinterestedness, in
that there is no immediate reward for them, make them perfect
witnesses to the presence of the invisible God.

Walking away from it all
It is not unusual that believers experience the temptation to
walk away from their belief in God. For some, there is hardly a
waking moment that is not badgered by the appeal of unbelief.
They say that there is no peace from voices, internal or external
to themselves, that mock at every choice in faith that they make
and that challenge every genuine manifestation of their religion.
There are those who have experienced God only in terms of a
life-long struggle of this kind.

Yet, we should also be aware that the tendency to doubt, including doubting matters that have to do with faith, is part of
the operation of a healthy mind. It would be a mistake to characterise all doubt as some kind of temptation. Doubt might equally
be an opportunity. All development and growth has an intellectual accompaniment that is shaped by questioning and by sincere doubt.

The challenges to religious belief in a person can frequently
present themselves as a kind of 'growing up' or 'coming of age'

experience. It could be that someone in quite a mature way realises that some of the stage-props of religious truth have simply fallen away. For example, a child may believe unquestioningly in the goodness and holiness of his or her parents, or have an absolute confidence in the goodness and holiness of the priest. In adulthood, such a person may have to cope with the loss of some of these impressions. Or it could be that a person has become disenchanted with views of the world in general that dominated his or her childhood, and now he or she is flooded with doubt as to what is really the case.

Suzanne has vivid memories of her teenage years, where the emphasis in her peer group was on how you would distance yourself from your parents and acquire a sense of your own individuality. For her and her companions, religion was an obvious area where difference could be experienced and tested:

> ... when I was about thirteen or fourteen, I suppose; the age when one starts to ask questions, and rebel, the usual things. When I was a teenager, you would have still lied to your parents that you were going to Mass ... you would have gone to a friend's house, hung around the freezing cold school sheds, rather than go into a nice warm church, because it wasn't cool to go into the church. And it was the age when you'd have amazingly wonderful conversations about God and Jesus and religion ... only sixteen year olds can be that confident about life really. But I would still see my parents as a source of ... what's the word ... guidance, or minding, or parenting in the church.

When she went to university, Suzanne's distance from the religion of her parents became more fixed and more stable:

> Going through college I studied social science, so obviously we'd have done a fair bit of sociology and philosophy. I suppose I'm always saying that when I find the time I'll read again, but I never could. Some friends of mine would reject Catholicism, as in the Mass on Sundays, 'apple pie' Catholicism, but they might be very spiritual people or they'd claim that they are very spiritual. I used to feel I am not very spiritual at all, actually.

It was at about this time that she encountered an important spiritual crisis:

My grandfather died, and he had lived with us and we were very close. My mother drew great comfort from his death. For our mother, he was re-united with his wife and they would all be together. Whereas I just felt a huge anger ... I was about nineteen at the time ... and I remember one night in the dark saying: 'Right, right, if there's a heaven, if you are out there, let me know ... now ... I want a sign ...' and of course, you don't get a sign. And I remember feeling very frustrated ... where does the life go? And not being happy with the answers that were available ... and I suppose that would sum up where I am, because I don't go out of my way to find out alternative answers. Where does the life go? Logically, you would say, the life is reborn into other life. If you look at plant life, plants die, they rot, and they feed other plants. You move up the line, you say: 'So what happens when animals die, when humans die ...' And who knows? But life stops and life starts; and the intelligence, the emotions and all of those pieces that are more than the physical roots ... where is all that ... that is the great mystery.

The phenomenon of personal developmental growth, however, whereby cherished views are challenged, altered or rejected, do not always cause serious problems for our understanding of religious faith. It is important that false or childish impressions of God be discarded. Many things alter as we grow up. It is natural to feel some distance from parents, family and home. The very process of taking to the world as an adult means having to discover anew who and what one is, and who and what one wants to be. We would naturally expect as much to happen with our religious views; it certainly happens with much else.

Belief in God is something that has to be looked at again in adulthood, and embraced or indeed rejected. It could be that a person simply walks free of those impressions that dominated his or her earlier life. It does happen that people walk away from faith in adulthood. The whole concept of human freedom that is central to Christian doctrine ensures that this possibility be recognised and accepted. Declan describes very well that moment when he chose to walk away from the faith world in which, by his own account, he had quite happily grown up. I had asked him about his childhood understanding of the origins of the universe:

> *Well, like every Irish boy born in the thirties, in the first part of my life that question would never have arisen, would certainly never have occurred to me, never did occur to me. So, up to the age of my early twenties, this was all very clear ... and, of course, 'who made the world?' ... 'God made the world' ... end of story.*

However, other ways of looking at things only became evident when he left home:

> *Then in my early twenties, when I was taken outside of the Irish environment ... then this question did occur to me. I had never been able to get answers to it ... but certainly the explanation I had up to that point, seemed to me ... suspiciously simple ... and the more I thought about it, in fact, very quickly, it began to appear almost absurd. This was in my early twenties, and I am now in my sixties and my views on the basic question haven't changed very much since then. This, this 'pat' explanation wasn't only a little bit suspicious, but really quite absurd, quite frankly, and I have never changed in my views about that particular issue since then.*

Suzanne and Declan speak above of their experiences of belief and unbelief in growing up and in adulthood. The 'temptation to walk away from it all' is not confined to the process of becoming an adult. There are many times in a person's life when holding on to faith in God challenges the believer to the utmost. For Martin, as we have seen, this is an ongoing experience.

The history of salvation is predicated on the free will of every participant in that salvation. In fact, the world of 'unbelief' that is everywhere around us, whether it is formally announced as such or not, is precisely the context in which genuine faith in God has always been pitched.

The example of ordinary people
The learning of the truths of religion for any individual depends directly on the existence and co-operation of other people. In a

matter that seems to relate us primarily to God, this dependence on the ways of others like us may come as a surprise. Yet so it is. Without the word of somebody else, I would know nothing about God or about Jesus Christ. This role of others in the more important aspects of our own lives can easily be overlooked. Whether it is my parents, or role models chosen by me, or somebody that just came to my notice because of what he or she really believed and practised, their influence in my own coming to believe can hardly be overestimated.

Each of us, moreover, learns about the world in a deeply personal fashion. This is such an obvious truism that it is very possible to overlook it also. Yet the passing on of the faith that we have received is a common task that depends totally, humanly speaking, on each one of us co-operating in our own way with the work of God. We cannot either begin to believe or make progress in faith without the assistance of our brothers and sisters.

All of this draws attention particularly to the sense of 'witness' that attends each person. We have to grasp the idea that the influence of each one plays a primary role in understanding the nature of Christian faith. The actual dynamic is not simply one of God revealing himself to men and women, although it is frequently assumed that this is the case. What takes place, when we look at it more closely, is that we are influenced by this or that person to look upon God in a particular way, whether it is in the compassion of another person, or his or her happiness, or peace, or hope, or in his or her perseverance in darkness or aridity. We begin to realise that there is no reason why that quality that speaks to us of God in another person could not also be our own. Hence a link is made between human example and the call of God.

In our conversation, Martin traced his faith quite simply to his own home and childhood:

It (my faith) probably comes from the family background. Even as a child I was very conscious of the importance of the local church in my education, in my growing up, and I would regularly visit the church.

When Paula spoke to me of her parents and of her grand-
mother, it was clear that she knew well how much she owed to
each of these for her present understanding of God. A seemingly
strict upbringing, humorously recollected, has convinced her of
this:

> *My Dad and my Mam. Sunday mornings if you missed Mass in
> our house there'd be murder. I lived with my Granny, and my
> Granny would have been from the old stock, which was, if you
> missed the first reading, you had to stay for that Mass and stay all
> for the next Mass, and I hated going to Mass ... and they always
> made sure.*
>
> *My Dad brought us up ... my Dad's a devout Catholic ... he
> would be the one that on Sunday would say to us: 'Did you go to
> Mass?' If you missed Mass, or if you got dolled up even going to
> Mass, he used to give out to us because he used to say: 'You're not
> going to Mass for a fashion parade ... you go to Mass to pray...' He
> would be the one that had brought me up to believe the way I be-
> lieve.*[8]

Yet Declan is equally sure that he thinks differently from
other members of his family and differently from many of his
friends. I asked him whether, in his own experience of growing
up, there had been anything like role models, people to whom
he felt drawn because of what they had been, what they had
done. I wondered whether the idea of independence of mind, of
a person who questions things, of one that takes a road not chosen
by many, had any special appeal to him:

> *Certainly not in my family ... to this day there are members of my
> family with whom I wouldn't discuss these issues. I don't know
> what they think I believe in. I have a brother who is a priest ... a per-
> son with whom you might say I should discuss these things ... I
> never would. For a long time I did admire people who would be seen*

---

8. Paula's experience of her father in this matter is very different from
that of both Suzanne and Martin. In Ireland religious matters in the
home have often been seen as the province of the mother. See Tom
Inglis, *Moral Monopoly, The Rise and Fall of the Catholic Church in Modern
Ireland*, Dublin, 1998, pp 146, 196.

as the intellectuals of the church ... but ... when I threw away the system, of course, I threw away the bearers at the same time. The people I admire are the people who would be radical ... in retrospect, I admire Martin Luther, although I don't believe his belief ... I like people like Darwin. While I was nurtured a Catholic, I am by instinct a Protestant, and by conviction an atheist ... in that I like being given to question things in a very gentle, civilised manner ... and I don't go and beat other people around the head when they come back with different answers. That I admire ... so if you were to ask me is there anyone to whom I am ... a disciple, certainly not ...

Notice that while Declan says he is not a disciple of anyone, yet he also acknowledges some of the people whom he admires, like Martin Luther and Charles Darwin. All I want to show here is the way in which those whom we admire can influence each of us. This influence is always an important factor in matters of belief, whether religious or secular. Although he is a non-believer in the religious sense, Declan is no exception to this very ordinary rule.

Notice also what he calls his 'very gentle, civilised manner'. There is something important here. Atheists are not the only people who can be criticised on occasion for intolerance. The church has suffered much from a time when religious teaching was characterised by phrases like 'he had the faith beaten into him'.

Life is a school in which we advance with the knocks and reversals that come our way as well as with the rewards. As we progress through life, our intellectual grasp of things matures. As more things are seen and learned, those things that we thought we understood well enough are seen in a new light. The reflective person is constantly 'tuning in' to new levels both of questions and of answers. He or she is picking things up for the first time, expanding his or her knowledge and understanding, recognising things not perceived in the same way before. With increasing familiarity and subtlety, the listening mind gradually builds up impressions of religious belief that help to unravel somewhat the mystery that surrounds it.

Martin provides an interesting example of this kind of progress or maturation in thinking. We were talking about a lifetime much of which was spent with books. By the age of eight, for example, on his own reckoning, he had already read most of Dickens and, as an adult, had read very widely in modern English, French, American, Russian and Irish literature. Early on in our conversation, he had mentioned that he had always been attracted by the faith and holiness of St Thérèse of Lisieux, a young French Carmelite nun. Towards the end, however, he mentioned that he now found it impossible to re-read the autobiography of Thérèse:

> But I was just thinking … how your tastes change, for example … I was talking a lot earlier on about Thérèse, the Little Flower, and her book 'The Story of a Soul' impressed me so much when I first read it. Then, some years ago, I went back to reading it again … a thing you should never do. I couldn't finish it, in fact I couldn't even get half way through it, I gave it up because I found it so naïve and so childlike almost … I'd say almost childish … in its approach to so many things. And I felt that this is so much out of character with the woman whom I know to be such an extraordinarily courageous and strong woman that it's presenting a false picture … so I gave it up rather than to lose my hold on the essential Thérèse.

It seemed Martin was touching on something quite significant here. Once you feel you have seized something important in a person, then you subsequently hold on to that importance rather than allowing even the person's own writing, or their public *persona*, to take it from you …

> I mean at fifteen years of age to go into a convent is one thing and to be obsessed with the notion of serving God … but to spend the following nine years in darkness … that's an extraordinarily heroic thing … and she kept saying: 'even if he should kill me, I would still believe in him …' and that about sums up my feelings, many times during my life … 'even if you kill me, I'll still hang on'.

Martin's reflection shows the profound significance of the influence of others on our personal development, including our

faith development. Examples of ordinary people having such influence are widespread in the New Testament. The gospel of St
John tells us the story of the Samaritan woman and the role she
played in bringing others to Jesus and to God. Here is the closing scene of a longer narrative:

> *Many of the Samaritans of that town had believed in him on the*
> *strength of the woman's testimony when she said, 'He told me all*
> *that I had ever done', so, when the Samaritans came up to him, they*
> *begged him to stay with them. He stayed for two days, and when he*
> *spoke to them many more came to believe; and they said to the*
> *woman, 'Now we no longer believe because of what you told us; we*
> *have heard him ourselves and we know that he really is the saviour*
> *of the world'.*[9]

The influence the martyr, Stephen, had on the young Saul is
another example. His story is to be found in the Acts of the
Apostles.[10] Stephen was brought before the High Priest in
Jerusalem and charged with a crime not too different from that
with which Jesus had been charged. He had said, apparently,
that God did not live in any kind of house or in any kind of temple. We can still read his speech today as it was written down
after his trial.

Stephen died for his own witness to the revelation of God.
His composure at his trial and his bearing at his death made a
deep impression on the young Saul, later St Paul, who was present and consenting to his death. Stephen was the first martyr of
the Christian faith, and his influence lives with us still.

Sooner or later, Christians believe, however, reflection goes
beyond what has been received from others. It leads beyond
human contact and human knowledge to the presence of the
One who has created us and who communicates with us. Yet it is
another human being who always stimulates the first movement
in the path that leads us to God. We need to keep this human dimension constantly in mind. Religious belief is a phenomenon
of human community.

---

9. John 4:29-32.
10. For the full account of Stephen's trial and death, see Acts 6:8-8.1.

CHAPTER TWO

Faith is from God

Faith in God comes to us first from other people. This is how all belief, conviction and knowledge is shaped. Yet, it also becomes clear that this design is one that originates in God. Faith is in every case a gift from God. How this can be is the theme of the present chapter.

The normal or natural condition of people is one that is constantly in touch with imaginative pictures that attempt to make sense of the world. For the most part, it would seem that people seek to believe in what comforts them and re-assures them. For many thousands of years, the general drift of such belief was in the direction of vague 'divine' entities, usually modelled on perceptions of the human condition. Examples can be seen in historical books or on a visit to a museum of comparative religion.

Then the view took hold that a definite call of some kind became registered in the human psyche, a call that originated outside of the human condition, coming to it from beyond space and beyond time. This view took place in the Middle East. The view is associated with the three main monotheistic religions in the world, namely Judaism, Christianity and Islam.

In more modern times, an opposite view has emerged: that there is nothing 'out there'. The view that there is no 'God' has been taking hold of human consciousness. It is alleged that human autonomy and dignity lies in the recognition and acceptance of this 'fact'. It is a view that is associated particularly with Western Europe.

According to monotheistic belief, knowledge of the one God is really available to us because God has revealed himself to us. Christians believe that such knowledge is always a gift on the part of God. Their belief is that this same God of the Jews has entered human history by becoming a human being, Jesus Christ of Nazareth. In other words, there is a dimension that is from inside the universe as well as a dimension that comes from outside. From a Christian perspective, this same Jesus is the key to all history; he is at once responsible for the creation and for the redemption of the world.

The Jewish faith continues to believe in Abraham, Moses and the Prophets, as well as in the sacred history of their people, as they did at the time of Jesus. While there is a growing movement of Jews that wishes also to claim Jesus, the Jewish religion as a whole does not accept him. Islam does accept Jesus as a prophet of God; but it does not accept the exclusive claims for Christianity that are made by Christians. For the Muslim, the great prophet of God is Mohammed who lived in the ninth century AD.

The Jews were the first people to believe that there was a single personal God. This perspective is one that developed in the land-bridge between Europe and Asia, beginning sometime about 2,000 BC.

My purpose in this chapter is simply to state what it is that Christians believe about the 'giftedness' of faith in God. It is not a question of trying to prove that God exists. If that could be proven definitively, as in a geometric proof for example, then it would no longer be *open* to any person to either embrace or reject it. This freedom on the part of the person to embrace or reject belief is a very important and necessary constituent of human action according to the Christian view. The chapter is written with God largely in the foreground, not in the background. His initiative, that is his taking the first step, is the first and most vital point to be understood about the Christian understanding of faith.

Faith is always a gift – a gift that invites goodness. Each of us, man and woman, is primarily called by God to become his or her best self. This call embraces all the possibilities of choice and limitation that may be set before us. It embraces the person in the home and in the workplace as well as in the wider community. It includes the skills and talents that an individual person may possess.

The Christian idea prioritises God the giver, not the human person who is the receiver of the gift. That idea distances the gift from human efforts and enquiries while not rejecting these completely. It takes the main emphasis of belief away from the intellectual and rational sphere. Faith, of course, does have an intellectual and a human component. But this component is one that responds to what has been already offered to us. This intellectual aspect is a response to the gift of God, a response that is made possible in every case by God's gift that is active in the person. Grace is simply another term for the 'gifting' of God.

Christians believe that unaided they cannot communicate with God. All communication with him, whether by an adult or by a child, requires some help from him, both in the initiation and in the carrying through of the communication. That is why faith is always described as a gift. A sincere unbeliever is simply unable for now to participate in communication with God, or has decided that such a communication is not real because of his or her belief that God does not exist.

However, in theory certainly, if not everywhere in practice, Christianity has always acknowledged the sincere belief of every person. This holds true where such belief is thought to be in error. In the overall providence of everything, this is an aspect of the divine will for each person.

Faith: a personal decision
In knowing God, the act of faith always precedes the knowledge that follows it. It is often called the venture of faith. This leap of faith is basically an act of trust in God whom we cannot see. In other words, to believe is to jump from what is known with the senses to what is known spiritually 'through' the senses. Every child normally makes that jump unconsciously. In adulthood, it often happens that the jump has to be taken again in a more deliberate fashion. The believing person moves from knowledge of what he sees and hears, sense knowledge of which he is certain, to a conclusion prompted only in part by that sense knowledge. The main part of the prompt comes, we believe, from God.

The knowledge of God that Christians talk about is a matter of personal judgement based on a reading or on an appreciation of the evidence that is experienced. In other words, while it is a most reasonable act to believe, reason itself does not compel belief; it does not dictate that we have to believe. Reason permits belief. Reason prepares the mind for the act of faith whereby one believes, but that act of faith is a move beyond reason, a move that is based not so much on reason as on trust. In a process like this, reason only takes a person so far; personal judgement and commitment are critical to gaining truth.

There was a telling illustration of the 'non-compelling' evidence of natural things, the things we can know through reason, in my conversations with Martin and Suzanne. Martin and I had been talking about ways in which God could be seen as more believable. We live in an age where people constantly say 'show it to me', but you cannot show them God directly. What is it about faith in God, I asked Martin, that it is only when you become really aware of it, it becomes obvious?

I really don't know how you convince people of the existence of a power, over and beyond our own knowledge of events and things, except by looking at the world around you, looking at nature, looking at flowers. I find that as I get older I become more conscious of the extraordinary beauty of a single flower. I mean, I think for example of Monet painting his lilies in his garden, how each flower, each lily, became an object of veneration to him. It's only by recognising the beauty of each single flower ... you begin to marvel at how did this happen, where did all these hundreds of daisies that spring up in the lawn and which we cut down with our lawnmowers, each of them is a little gem, where did they come from, who composed them? You are talking about the beauty of music or of literature, which are marvellous, yet no piece of music, no piece of literature, can achieve the beauty of a single petal. You look at a rose, for example, petal upon petal upon petal, how could it have happened, where did it come from, and you have to start going back to an original cause somewhere. There must have been something out there that brought this into being.

Yet Suzanne, unlike Martin, felt quite unmoved at this level by the existence of flowers. We had been talking about the possibility of there being a God:

I don't see that there's a possibility. I think it's too simplistic to say that there is a God who is a person who cares about us all and is minding us all individually when you see what happens in the world. The natural disasters that happen in the world, for example, are part of some kind of order that keeps the world in balance. So there is something outside of us that we don't know about … whether we are part of some great scientific explosion … whether we are a moment of time within a million years … whatever that means.[1] You just have to look at nature, why do the seeds grow, and why do the flowers grow, and why do babies get born … it happens. Now I don't think any religion has got it necessarily sorted; a religion is a group of people who have struggled with this and come up with a way of understanding it.

Martin and Suzanne highlight very different perceptions of flowers. They show how different people can find themselves at opposite ends of the spectrum on what are very ordinary issues.

Much of our assent to what we know tends to be passive, indifferent almost. We take it for granted. But with faith it is different. In faith, there is a personal engagement and commitment in the knowing that takes place. Faith in God calls for the kind of knowledge that is a conscious and willing participation in the events of life informed by that belief. A person who believes may not feel very differently from others at times, but he or she knows and cares about matters of faith. For example, such a person may be as distressed as others at the suffering that is in the world, but his or her distress is experienced within a God believing context that both challenges and consoles.

---

1. It should be pointed out that neither the possibility of us being the result of some vast explosion, nor that we are a moment of time within a million years, nor the fact that we are a part of nature, is in any way in contradiction with the act of faith. Most Christians who think about it today probably accept the first of these propositions, while they certainly accept the latter two.

It might well be objected that the very idea of faith is very convenient and that it masks some of the real difficulties and pressures of life. In my conversation with Suzanne, I had suggested that behind everything in the universe there was a kind and loving presence. Her reply was to the point:

You see, again, 'God being a kind, a strong and kind person.' It's a bit like when people used to say to me: 'I'd really like to work in personnel management because I really like people.' I worked in personnel and said 'you really shouldn't like people if you work in personnel because most of the things you do are actually not always pro the individual, they are pro the common good. So you might be making people redundant, or not promoting people, or not putting people in the job they should be in … you're just suiting the organisation.

For Suzanne, the idea of a general providence has the atmosphere of terror about it. The notion of one great God manipulating the world was a frightening one. The idea of his arranging an earthquake here or a war there in order to keep things under control seemed barbaric, as indeed it is.

Now where is the sense of 'individual loving God' in that? And can you have both, maybe you can, but I'm not sure. I can't reconcile that with children being bombed because they happen to be in a particular place, or the children in this country … the things you hear … that are no fault of individuals or their parents or their surroundings … they are just in the wrong place at the wrong time. But maybe the benevolence is not about the individual thing but is about the greater good.

In addition to the arbitrariness that might be associated with God, Suzanne saw it as a mistake to view life through a lens that might tend to favour God. In this she was partly right. It is a mistake to think of faith simply as a disposition or as a sunny outlook on life. A kind of natural optimism, or indeed pessimism, is neither here nor there when we are considering the act of faith. Once again, Suzanne drew me up sharply in our conversation. I had said that prayer, it seemed to me, was being aware. 'The experience on a spring day of simply being alive, the buds on the trees, the air … to me there is an element of faith in this; it is a kind of prayer …'

It's probably your 'serotonin' balance is up, and you're great ...

'Yes, but it fills into a whole larger picture ... I want to thank ...' I said.

Yes. I know what you mean. That lovely spring day, and you can smell the air and you feel: 'Yes, I'm so lucky to be alive'. Yes, I do know what you mean. I was just thinking there as you were talking, I suppose the accepted wisdom is that God is something out there, beyond the clouds, that it is one being, embracing all of us. I don't know that this is a philosophical thought, in any fashion anywhere ... but, supposing that it's actually somewhere within yourself, that there's a God inside all of us. Because you see there is a force within us to live a good life ... the natural human condition is to live and to help others live, so that does come from somewhere. Is it just part of our make up as humans, the way the stem is part of the daffodil, or is it something more than that? That's what is interesting ... because it is natural.

The flow of human life and culture already includes in its ordinary momentum many attitudes and dispositions, optimistic as well as pessimistic. These are normal, and in themselves they are not evidence of any special giftedness from God. These currents of opinion are all about us. They are a central aspect of the context in which ordinary life is lived. Without them it would be impossible to conceive of a human existence at all. What the gift of faith does do is to offer us a perspective from God that transforms our human understanding and in which we can share.

Faith: a whole way of life

One gets a sense from Martin's account of it that faith is deeply personal, is a whole way of life. It is not simply another judgement that there is a God, for example. Martin spoke later of the influence of St Thérèse on his life:

I won't say I model my life on her, but I model my attitude on Thérèse's vulnerability, her attitude. 'I'm nobody, I'm a little speck out here in the world, and you are, you are up there and you are all powerful, you can do anything and I can do nothing ... but the less I can do, the more you can do ...' It's like the other Thérèse, Teresa of Avila, who

said: 'When I'm at my weakest, I am most strong' ... and I've always
worked from that position because, I know it's a cowardly way out if
you like, I work on that position that I can't do a damn thing: 'I'm
lost, so please, don't let me down.' I know it may not have any great
theological basis or anything else, but I know it's the answer to a
whole lot of problems in life.

We find that St Paul often speaks of faith in this way. 'For God's foolishness is wiser than human wisdom, and God's weakness is stronger than human strength.'[2] There is a conscious irony here, as Paul draws attention to the overwhelming strength of God, evident in many ways but not always in human affairs as we approach them. Again we pick up the theme when Paul writes of the close affinity between the disciple and Christ: 'True, I am living here and now, this mortal life; but my real life is the faith I have in the Son of God, who loved me, and gave himself for me.'[3]

In listening to Paula's contrast between her own life and the life of Don, her husband, and his father, this theme of faith as a whole way of life also comes out very clearly, although expressed differently:

Don's father doesn't believe, and even Don ... I always say Don is
agnostic, he's sitting on a fence, he doesn't know which side he is on
... I mean it's probably the way he was reared. I think it's very sad,
very, very sad ... because even the time that Don's mother died I said,
'I'd go up and light a candle in the church; I'd ask people to say a
prayer for her; but, you have nothing.' I think it's very sad that no-
body has any belief, any faith ... because his father doesn't believe in
anything ...

Paula feels the contrast between her own way of life and that of her husband even though, as husband and wife, they are close to each other. Her relationship with God reassures her in the face of life's demands and uncertainties.

It is important to recognise that the gift of faith can play a significant part in resolving people's deeper questions about life. I

---

2. 1 Cor 1:25.
3. Gal 2:20.

don't want to assert that religious faith is the only way that such questions are resolved. We have seen that Suzanne and Declan have each found a measure of contentment in their choices. For the most part, as we know, people spend limited time agonising on fundamental questions. We do not normally sense a crisis about such issues as 'Who am I?', 'Why am I?', 'What happens when I die?', 'Is there a God?' The gift of faith, however, brings with it a great confidence in the face of questions like these.

What we find is that faith brings with it an ordinary certitude of the kind that most of us, including many unbelievers, hope for. As believers, we believe that we can 'hope against hope', as so often happens in life. Our faith assures us, in the words of the letter to the Hebrews, that there is substance to our hope, that what we hope for really exists but it is unseen.[4] This is Christian faith in its full maturity. St Paul speaks in one place of Christians who are still children, immature: 'who are tossed to and fro and carried about with every wind of doctrine'.[5] As an adult act of judgement, faith has a finality and a certainty that brings closure, at a speculative level, to ultimate issues that naturally trouble the mind, while leaving everything open to the great infinity that exists in and beyond all that is created.

Faith: a natural convergence
In the act of religious faith, we bring together in our minds many disparate facts, often unconsciously. We make a judgement about them that seems to transcend any one of them when taken singly. In other words, it seems that we approach the places where God may be found by virtue of a convergence of possibilities. A native hunter will identify thousands of pointers that will lead him to his prey, indications and little tell tales that are hidden to other minds.[6] A medical diagnosis often proceeds by a similar method. So too is a case built up in court. Theory and practice accompany each other in an identification of what the situation in dispute

4. Heb 11:1-3ff.
5. Eph 4:14.
6. All of these ideas are Newman's. See C. S. Dessain, *John Henry Newman*, (New Edition) Oxford, 1980, pp 177-158.

actually is. A ship's cable can illustrate what happens in the mind: individual strands that count for nothing on their own bring certitude when they are combined in a particular way.[7] So it is with faith.

The farmer sows his seed and tends it in the springtime, anticipating a good harvest in the autumn. That faculty of anticipation that allows us to predict from one day to the next that which is unseen illustrates this aspect of faith. Faith permits us to anticipate a whole present and future that will be different from the world that we know now. Faith may be accompanied by difficulties, confusion, darkness, but at its core is found confidence, optimism, and even certitude. It anticipates a future that will be very different to the present that we know here on earth. In this, of course, we have a danger as well as an opportunity. The danger is the temptation to overlook all the injustice that there is in the world and to say simply that it will be better in the future. The opportunity is the encouragement that faith gives to take the world seriously and to bring about some measure of change for the better in it.

The act of faith in God is complex and it has many aspects to it: attraction, wish, desire, possibility of a future, sense of personal fulfilment. As we have seen, 'trust' is a word that sums up this whole range of personal investment. To compare the act of trust in God with a person choosing a marriage partner illustrates something of what happens in religious faith. The comparison is both like and unlike at the same time. When a man proposes to a woman in marriage, the man trusts in his own judgement, and he trusts the woman whom he chooses, or who chooses him. And there's the catch! In a relationship of love with another person, the lover comes to love a person who is already there and who very possibly already loves him (or her), whether or not he (or she) knows it yet. It may be that the one thought of as the loved person loved first. In a relationship of faith with God, it is God, we believe, who loves first.

---

7. Newman, see: *The Letters and Diaries of John Henry Newman*, edited by C. S. Dessain, *et al*, vols i–xxxi, London 1961-1984; xxi, p 146.

Faith: recognition and trust

Let us consider the idea of recognition and trust in what we do. An essential quality of every person is what is called human dignity. By this is meant that essential worth, that essential importance, that attaches to each one of us. A human person is to be distinguished always from what is merely a thing, even a thing of very great value. In what does this difference consist, we might ask. We can compare the human being with other creatures from the animal world. They too live and play and hunt and they have a measure of cunning and intelligence. But they are essentially different from us. We can compare the human with a robot, where some measure of calculation and prediction is also present, perhaps greater and more sophisticated than calculation and prediction in human beings. Yet we know that robots are not human and that they cannot be.

In order to assert this unique value, moreover, the human being need not be idealised in any way. Men and women sometimes bring with them endless trouble, yet their value at this level of which we speak is undiminished. The human person is always a unique and priceless individual.

When we reflect on it, it is clear that there is no way of justifying the perception of this unique distinctness of the human person in a fully satisfactory manner that everybody can accept. You either see it, or you don't. If you see it, you see it because you have understood a million facts, seen and unseen, and you have drawn the inescapable conclusion that human beings have a unique dignity. A convergence of possibilities that we can hardly explain leads us to recognise and feel this unique respect for each other. This respect need not diminish the respect in which other creatures are held; yet it is a respect that is different in some essential way.

The freedom of the human individual is another such understanding. This idea of freedom is something that we readily comprehend: yet it cannot be pinned down by science. That is not a limitation of science.

To perceive something is an act of personal judgement. Yet the capacity that the believer has for the perception and recognition of his or her fellow human beings is not one that everybody finds compelling or convincing. Moreover, there are whole schools of thought that understand the human being deterministically, that is, as not being really free. In support of their view they cite the many hindrances to freedom that undoubtedly exist.

As we have seen, it ought not to be supposed that human judgements are always completely guaranteed by reason. If we look at modern political life, it is evident that there are often several possible readings of situations. Some people may quite legitimately argue that the state ought to do all that it can to support every citizen and that it should do this by raising taxes. Others may argue with an equal legitimacy that the best possibility will be obtained when the state holds back or desists from attempting to provide universally for all citizens. We can extend this example to that wider range of knowing that is associated with one's own place and country. We constantly make choices that owe not a little to very justifiable prejudices that are related to local and personal loyalties. Yet, although we might spend our lives in service of them, we would never pretend that such loyalties or preferences have some absolute truth-value.

Each of us has the capacity for perception and for judgement. What I want to show is that this capacity for the full recognition of other people as having dignity and being free is a door to religious faith. Like the evidence for dignity and freedom, evidence that points to the existence of some higher being that has created us lies all around us. It is there, even if for many it does not convince. One looks at the world and concludes 'there is a God'. This is how faith begins.

Religious faith: a 'cop out'

A sense of impatience with the whole notion of a faith perspective was evident in the discussion that I had with Declan. For him faith is a 'cop-out':

> Faith ... I regard ... let me say this absolutely bluntly to you ... as the great 'cop-out'. In the times when I was still 'within religion', if I can

put it like that ... when the hard questions arose to which there weren't answers, you were told ... well ... 'faith'. I don't suppose I'd have expressed it like that at the time, but at one level I could see in organised religion ... when it ran up against something it couldn't collar, then you had 'faith' ... and I didn't think of it then, but afterwards it occurred to me ... that's the greatest 'cop-out' of all time. One of the absurdities was ... that if there is this creator who is all mercy ... and who has picked us, this little 'infinitesimal' part of creation to be the focus for the creator of the universe, of the godhead ... the font of all wisdom, knowledge, charity ... and he put us here ... why did he put us here with all these ridiculous impediments ... that to know him we have to have 'faith'? I'm afraid I can find no answer to that whatsoever ... but it's really what I felt ... and what I still feel ... is the absurdity of the thing. So faith means very little to me, quite frankly.

I suppose it's easy for me to say that, since I find no need of belief. So that if I were pursuing it and was running up against ... maybe I would have faith. Just let me say I am totally happy for people who believe in something ... who have faith, and who don't damage other people, or other elements of creation. I don't want to proselytise them, I don't want to go and say that this is nonsensical, or whatever ... I've absolutely no need to do that. Quite honestly, I find it very hard to believe that obviously very intelligent, very educated, very learned people can live with this thing called faith. It is just as simple as that.

I think that the only response that one can make to this view, as a believer, is to look carefully at how the act of faith compares with other conclusions and mental states that we readily accept. We can see, as believers, that the act of faith is a valid response to ultimate questions that arise in human existence. But even those questions have first to be recognised and identified by us. For a person like Declan, the questions themselves seem to have mutated in some way. He uses the word 'linear' to describe the 'line' of progress from birth to death, but he clearly feels that this perspective is far too individualistic, too person centred, to give us a grasp on the complexities of life.

It is all here and now ... the past is almost a figment of our imagin-

ation ... that ... you see we are these linear, biological beings ... we are born, we come and we go ... We are so structured by our biological states ...

'You would say that the present moment is all there is ...' I asked.

Right. So we have this construct called the past, the present and the future ... if you want to get down to it ... All there is, is now ... and the past is an accumulation of facts and experiences, and all the rest of it ... and the future, which we worry about, all the time ... I mean, we can't know it, we don't know what's going to happen ... but in a way it's here now that everything that is going to happen is predicated ...

There are no 'unpredictables' in science, no 'miracles' in life, it seems. The circularity in Eastern religion, an acceptance that everything repeats, is wrapped up in a kind of 'eternal now':

Nothing miraculous happens ... nothing totally out of the order happens ... so, in a way, if you can just get your mind and stand back ... out of time, linearity and all the rest of it, and our own little three score and ten ... that everything is here now ... the way in nature, nothing is destroyed. I like the circularity within most of the eastern religions, certainly in Buddhism ... I think it is in Hinduism ... where really, the nearest approach we can get to it is a 'circularity' rather than a linearity ... and this is where I feel, I think, there is something that appeals to me in that.

I responded: 'You are putting your finger on something important when you talk about linearity and circularity ... this is where the Western religious tradition, that is Judaism, Christianity and Islam also, is based on a belief that at a certain stage there *was* a miracle ... at a certain stage someone did cut in, broke the flow, and this voice called Abraham to leave his country, his family and his fathers house, 'for the land I will show you'.[8] At a subsequent stage that same personage gave to Moses his name, as 'I am who I am'.[9] That is the big difference ... that in

---

8. Gen 12:1-9.
9. Ex 3:13-15 & par.

the Western tradition religion is actually historical, it dates from a particular time and it progresses from there ... and that its history is very real. It not only began at a time and place in the world, but it is heading towards some kind of ultimate conclusion, in which all Christians trust. That is ultimately what Christian faith is about ... whether you can accept that such a thing is possible, or can accept that it did happen. Or you find yourself saying 'I don't believe that happened; I don't believe it could happen.' In reply, Declan disagreed:

> I don't want to sound offensive ... I think of this 'almighty God ...' why does he have to get up to conjuring tricks ... to convince us ... And these great people in religious belief ... Abraham, Jesus, Mohammed ... I don't know that much about Abraham, or about Mohammed ... but if you take Jesus ... this whole thing about 'the son of God' ... 'God made man, dying for our sins, redeeming us ...' On a literary, dramatic level ... this is fantastic, it is really wonderful ... but to me it is myth ... like myths from other places and religions. Jesus existed obviously ... and I mean, as a moral philosopher, fantastic, absolutely fantastic ... my God, when I see what's grown out of him ... the poor man, is all I would say ... but it happens to all of these great people. Buddha, you look at Buddhism, now it is riven with conflicts and strictures and all kinds of things ... He preaches, as far as I can see, a simple the most acceptable things I have heard from any figure ... I know Buddhism is not a religion ... it's quasi philosophy I suppose ... but it's a way of seeing things ... and I think that's what I like ... I don't believe that there is a supernatural being who created all of this ... that we are playthings in his scheme ... I don't believe that at all.

We might notice that with the disappearance of a certain 'linearity' in our thinking, a linearity that connects both the past and the future, each of these – past and future – move out of sight. It would seem that the 'common sense' view of reality that underpins ordinary life in our culture depends more than is realised on assumptions that are linked to faith in God. The continued existence in some sense of the past, for example, or the normal and confident prediction that there will be a future, are two pillars on which all of science, law and commerce are built. We don't usually think of these areas as ones that require proof in order to be accepted.

Yet if we continue to dismantle the ordinary structure of our received thinking, the very foundations of our civilisation come up for examination. I am not saying that this should be considered as necessarily a bad thing. Nor do I want to discredit the value of certain perspectives on reality that bring out the transience of it. But we should notice the extent to which the 'giftedness' of our faith penetrates the giftedness of life. The gift of life includes, we believe, the gift of time, of past, present and future. That gifted faith tells us that all that we have, we have received from our Creator; it is not of our own making, and it is not the accident of some 'present' moment, however we might conceive of that moment. This is so even when God is not known or recognised, and even as his existence cannot be proven at the bar of science. The world as it has emerged in the Christian view is one that can be readily accepted and lived in. This is one of the, for now, temporary benefits of Christian civilisation.

However, with the disappearance of the very questions that religion poses, a whole new texture of social life faces us. It could happen that misleading impressions and generalisations about life and civilisation itself will begin to appear with the eclipse of the actual faith that underpins this system. In such conditions, the whole system may become unstable and we will face a less certain future.

It could happen that in the future the church view will be a minority one that is shared by a small number of adherents. A hundred years ago, for better and for worse, men and women in Western societies were born into a world where the doctrines of religion were considered to be public facts. A hundred years from now, it may be that men and women will be born into a world where the public significance of religion will be mainly archaeological in nature. On the other hand, in the world of Islam, where a public practice of faith is actively encouraged, it may be that things will work out differently. While this religion presents very different and divergent ways of understanding matters that in Christianity are considered basic to an understanding of God, nonetheless, Christians have much to learn from Islam, and much to share with those who follow the Qur'an.

Knowing God

Many years ago, when I was a teenager, the father of one of my companions introduced me to the music of Dvorak. I can still see the record in his hands; it was 'Symphony from the New World'. What he said to me was: 'If you want to understand a piece of music, you must listen to it again, and again, and again.' It has seemed to me ever since that there was something archetypal about this advice. The idea of engaging with something that might initially mean nothing was a kind of 'believing in order to understand'.

Music belongs to a realm of things that cannot be proven to be right or true. The kind of measurable criteria that are essential to progress in geometry, for example, are no use here. Nor are the logical deductions that can be so important in philosophical thought. Appreciating music has more to do with liking it than with quantity or with verification. If you find that you like the New World Symphony, then you enter a domain that is shared by many, but which can only be entered freely and without any force, even intellectual force. There is no compulsion in liking music. If the music is unfamiliar, then, by listening to it again and again, you may find yourself entering a new universe, a new understanding or knowing of unfamiliar melodies and rhythms.

Knowing God is something like this. At one level, from the human point of view, it can be said that God is completely unknown and unknowable. Yet in a seeming paradox, it can also be said that the way we come to know God is similar to the way we come to know any person. We come to know 'him' by being introduced to him, so to speak. Unfamiliarity gives way to a greater familiarity. Knowing a person can lead on to friendship with him or her, or to love. On our part, it can also lead to indifference or to enmity. This also happens in relation to God.

We recognise and know other persons differently from the way that we know facts. Knowing a person involves more than the rational faculties that we bring to bear on facts. My knowledge of my late father and mother, for example, draws on many levels of my awareness in relationship to them. It is an emotional knowing as well as a rational one, and it is a knowing that is borne out of my very own existence. By that I mean that it derives from the unique person that I am, it is not in any way a general or an abstract kind of knowledge. It is concrete and is rooted in the particularity, the individuality, of me. This includes the reality of my shared existence with brothers and a sister, and many impressions received over the years from the wider world. All of our deeper personal knowledge of other people is like this. Most of us would readily admit also that not all of the levels of this 'knowledge' are easily or even completely available to us. Our preferences and our prejudices, after all, begin to be laid down long before we are conscious of them as such.

With hindsight, of course, the person who is a believer has an awareness of some kind of assistance given by God in the act of coming to know him. This assistance is called 'grace', which means 'gift', 'freely given'. Grace apart, what I want to show is that our knowing of God is subject to the same ground rules as our knowing of persons in general, as well as our knowing of facts. For the most part, we know people and things because others bring us to them or tell us about them. For the most part, we recognise the giftedness of much of that basic, even unconscious, knowledge that we have imbibed from others since our own beginning. We have seen for ourselves that this knowledge is reliable and we have learned to trust our own judgement about it. We trust our own judgement, even as we know that we can be deceived by that same judgement. It is this same process that leads us to faith in God and to the recognition that faith is from God.

CHAPTER THREE

Faith and Conscience

In this chapter I want to show the critical connection that exists between faith and conscience. Faith, being the gift of God, comes from a source that cannot be examined directly. The believer receives the gift graciously and on trust. Yet without conscience there cannot be faith, because conscience provides an important awareness upon which the act of faith is based. We begin with a brief examination of what is meant by conscience.

The idea of conscience

Conscience is usually defined as a faculty of the mind that distinguishes between right and wrong, and that influences conduct accordingly.[1] The distinction between right and wrong is a moral one. A disposition to do right in a person is one of good moral character.

Initially, we each seem to pick up from our parents a sense of what doing right is and that it will be vindicated eventually. It seems that most people start off with this basic formation. The conscience of a child is not preserved from error, any more than that of an adult. As we grow older, we may become critical of what we have already learned in childhood. At this stage, conscience may be revised or reformed in line with new awareness and new knowledge.

When I say that we each have a sense of what is right and wrong, at least to start with, I refer in the first place to a natural feeling that flows both from what we are and from what we have learned. It is a feeling that ordinary social and political life relies upon completely.

---

1. *The Pocket Oxford Dictionary*, op. cit., p 165.

Traditionally, the faculty of conscience (or the lack of it) has been linked to the presence (or absence) of God in the soul. In modern times, the idea that God is linked to conscience has been severely undermined, as well as the notion that conscience gives access to any valid knowledge of right and wrong. As an example of views in this vein, conscience is often thought of more as a kind of conditioned or programmed response that relates to inhibitions picked up in childhood, a response that can be grown out of in adulthood.

The view persists in most people that they know the difference between right and wrong, even if they move away from Christian belief. Both in religious and secular thought, there is a fair degree of certainty among people about these matters. While the traditional notions of conscience that were once widely held have been interrogated thoroughly in modern times, it has not dislodged the basic conviction of the ordinary person that distinguishes right from wrong.

Conscience, which includes moral thought, is often experienced as a kind of feeling. Our feelings are aspects of human awareness that belong to the interaction between the individual and his or her environment. Moral feeling is connected to the mind. It often seems that we can know with certainty when we see right and when we see wrong. We would stake our life on it and, for the most part, we think we would be right.

For the believer, moral thought runs side by side with the thought that God exists. This thought that God exists is usually, although not always, accompanied by a sense of the presence of God. We believe that God infuses this awareness of his presence. In other words, believers understand that conscience is a gift from God that signals his actual presence to the person.[2]

For Christians, the phenomenon that is called conscience is

2. The predominant emphasis in Newman's description of conscience was a sense of the presence of God. See, for example, *Parochial and Plain Sermons*, 1832 & ff. (Vol 1), Sermon 2 *The Immortality of the Soul*, and Sermon 15 *Religious Faith Rational; University Sermons*, op. cit., Sermon II, op. cit., pp 18-20; *Grammar of Assent* (1870) chapt. 5. 1. *Belief in God*, pp 95-109.

one that touches on faith perceptions and on moral perceptions at the same time and in the same way. It appears that a consciousness of God and a consciousness of what goodness means go together in the human psyche. But the link with God, we believe, can also be lost. It appears then that 'the gift' whereby we associate God with the knowledge of right and wrong is replaced by something that is simply our own opinion on the matter.

The Christian idea of conscience, then, refers to an actual presence of God to each person. It is this presence, Christians assert, that gives a guaranteed access to a sense of right and wrong.

The moral judgement

The world is one in which every man and woman silently discriminates between good and bad behaviour. People know intuitively what is right, in broad strokes admittedly. Our knowledge of morals is something that we can put our hands on, so to speak, without much hesitation. It is a knowledge that is real and very direct. We know frequently, although not always, when we see right and when we see wrong.

Paula was very clear on the difference between right and wrong and on the fact that everybody knows this difference in some way. I suggested to her the Ten Commandments[3] as a starting point for our conversation about morality:

Yes ... I would know them ... but don't ask me to write them all out for you (laughing) ... I learned them as a rhyme ... yes I do ...

'These aspects of religion that have to do with doing things ... not necessarily going to church or that ... but with the kind of person you are ... the kind of values you have ... talk to me a little about that', I asked her.

I can only do my best ... at the end of the day ... I know I've done loads wrong in my life ... and that's what confession is for, to go and say I'm sorry ... and I live by the commandments ...

---

3. See Ex 20:1-17; Deut 5:1-22.

'How do you know you have done wrong? Is it because you have gone against something you have been told, or is it something deeper in yourself?'

It's something I KNOW that I've done wrong … not that I've been told … I mean everybody knows right from wrong. There are things I've done … I mean, stupid things … I have done things wrong in my life … the same as everybody on this earth. I know most people feel badly when they have done wrong.

'Do you think that you depend on your religion for that … knowing right from wrong … or would you know anyway?'

I would know anyway, but religion helps. I was also told by school, family, priests … by loads of people … what was right and wrong. It kind of all combines … in together … everybody working together to tell you: 'This is the way you are supposed to live … if you do this, it is wrong.' Plus the fact that you have the feeling … you know yourself … you do know yourself, no matter what you do, you know what's right or wrong.

'And, as you say, you know …'

You do know, deep inside you do know if you've done something wrong … you do know, no matter what happens … or no matter how bad or how good you are, or whether you have religion or whether you have no religion, you do know …

We pick up here again a strong reflexive note on Paula's part, as we have already noted in my conversation with Martin. It is as if she knows that she knows, but cannot explain it further. I asked her whether people who didn't believe in God have moral knowledge to the same extent as those who did believe:

I wouldn't be able to answer that. They do have their morals. I know from Don's father, and he knows right from wrong … and he taught them right from wrong. He was taught right from wrong … and his family were atheists as well … so he was taught right from wrong … so with them, I'd say it's come from a family, whereas we're getting it from a group of people … you know, we are getting it from the church, family … police, like we're getting it from everybody.

Suzanne brings to her understanding of morality a wish for order as opposed to chaos, so much so that she even goes to church with her children on Sundays and has them enrolled in a multi-denominational religious school, even though she herself does not believe in God at this point of her life:

My kids go to a multi-denominational school. I think it's very important that they learn the full range ... and have at least a basis on which to make choices. But I also wanted them to learn the Catholic religion, which they do. My daughter has made her first communion, and I feel like a bit of a hypocrite actually, in the preparation for the communion, teaching the material we're supposed to teach. At the same time I think ... when you see kids who are in a vacuum, who have nothing to actually consider. They should at least have some basis on which to figure out life.

'So what's coming across is the idea of values, order, because society requires order ...'

I think increasingly society requires order, and I think the Catholic religion probably provided that in Ireland back in the forties and fifties and the early sixties. People of my generation were brought up with that order. I would worry that the generation of kids of my friends don't have that structure at all. I don't know where they are going to get their rules from ... rules in the best sense, where are they going to get their benchmarks ... whatever language you want to use. There needs to be some set of norms. Just as simple as that, cultural and social norms that people can accept or reject or live around. But I worry about the sort of almost anarchic kind of situations when you see kids on TV and they just have no sense of the morality that we would have had, whether its religious based or not.

'Would it be correct to say that your appreciation of the value system, to a certain extent, comes out of your study of sociology?'

Probably partly ... my studying sociology was a result of my being interested in the whole idea of society: how it works and how people end up being how they are ... from the sociological point of view. But that's just one aspect that I find myself thinking about. Some of my friends laugh at me and say: 'You were the great rebel ... back

in your teens ... now you're the only one of us who has a child at
Mass every Sunday ...'

Declan is equally sure of his moral awareness and of his
knowledge of right and wrong. As he sees it, it is a kind of innate
knowledge in humans and even, in some manner of speaking, in
animals as well:

Absolutely ... absolutely ... I think these are almost self evident ...
but I can see no reason to have another supernatural rationale for
having moral views. If there is right there has to be wrong ... be-
cause you couldn't deal with the concept of right without wrong,
everything is this dichotomy. If you have good, you always have to
have evil, by definition ... so I require absolutely no set of com-
mandments to be handed to me to tell me what to do. I'm not saying
I am a good person. I hope ... I think there is an innate something in
people that ... more people are good ... there are more good people
than evil people. I think there are some ghastly evil people ... I don't
know why there are such evil people, but I think there is an innate
goodness in people.

To summarise these three views: Paula clearly expresses the
popular awareness of moral knowledge, not only on the part of
religious people, but also on the part of non-believers as well.
She is convinced that she is helped in this by her religion as well
as by other influences in her life; she is equally convinced that
her husband, who is not a believer, also knows right from
wrong. Suzanne links her knowledge of right and wrong to a desire for order in society; she is anxious about the anarchic element that can arise when there is no order. For Declan, right and
wrong are almost self evident; he thinks there may be an innate
goodness in most people.

Good and Evil

To set the scene, I would like to appeal to one of the lesser-
known plays of William Shakespeare, *Measure for Measure*. As
the action of this play unfolds, the 'duke' character makes it appear that he is going to be away for some time and he confers all

the rights of government on a deputy whom he enjoins to rule in
his absence with full powers of state. As the play develops, the
deputy becomes a fierce and unscrupulous despot. The duke,
however, does not go abroad. He assumes the disguise of a holy
friar and eavesdrops on all that is happening in the city during
his supposed absence. As a friar, he brings guidance and hope to
several people who are suffering under the misrule of his
deputy. In the final act, the denouement of the play sees the return of the duke, the vindication of the aggrieved, and 'just
deserts' meted out to the real villains of the piece, notably the
deputy and the character Lucio.

As I see it, the plot may be interpreted as a metaphor for the
situation in which we find ourselves in real life. This may or may
not have been Shakespeare's view. The duke can be seen as a figure of the God who will one day return and vindicate all who
have suffered in the wrong.[4] In his guise as a good friar, the
duke is shown as being fully aware of each injustice and grief
that happens during the action, although his real identity is hidden. In this manner, he is presented as being close to those who
are suffering unjustly. A sharp distinction is made between
what is moral and what is legal, and the script keeps the audience ever mindful of this distinction. All of the moral themes
that are explored in the play contrast with the legal situation that
exists and that weighs heavily on the people. Counted among
these themes are truthfulness and lying, chastity and lechery,
constancy and infidelity, as well as several others. The denouement, while painful for the villains, is yet mild and wonderful
for them as well, although not it seems for Lucio who resists
even his comic punishment at the end.

What interests me particularly about the play is the fact that
the audience is presumed never to be in doubt as to the moral
standing of each character. We know instinctively the good from

---

4. According to J. W. Lever, *Measure For Measure*, The Arden
Shakespeare, London 1965 (2002), lv-xcviii, it is likely that the author intended the play to reflect the concerns of people who were looking to
the new king, James I, to rule justly and well. The title however may be
traceable to the New Testament, Mt 7:1-3.

the bad, even though some of the good characters may appear to be compromised by their actions. In normal circumstances we are rarely unsure at this level, although we may differ with each other on how we perceive other aspects of the plot. We may well wonder how it is that we can have such certainty, when there is so much in our lives of which we know we cannot be sure.

Measure for Measure does not make any explicit connection with an idea of God as a ruler whose 'eyes and ears' are everywhere, and who will one day return to vindicate all of those who have suffered at the hands of others. The plot simply shows a prince in disguise moving among his people while they suppose that he is abroad. Yet the whole feeling of the play is very close to that feeling that Christians have (and others too) when they give thanks to God for the world, and when they pray that they be delivered from evil, including the evil that is within themselves. Such people believe that God is silently present to them everywhere and in everything, in good times as well as in bad. For such people, the opinion of their fellow men and women, in the last analysis, fades completely before God's view (or an eternal view) of what has been done or omitted.

Good and evil, for the person in the street, turn on something very like the existence of an unseen ruler who will one day return and vindicate those who have been wronged by people who have pretended to act in his name. The need for this vindication is something that many people feel in their bones. Shakespeare, however he intended the character of the duke to be read, was tapping into something very fundamental and very human in the plot of this play. The scriptures, the Old and New Testaments, are replete with imagery of this kind and with a sense of justice that corresponds exactly to this feeling. In the scriptures, there are many invocations of God as an unseen father who is always with us. At least two of the parables of Jesus speak of an absent king whose son is violently abused and put to death unjustly.[5] But in the end justice will be sure.

5. Mt 25:14-15, and Lk 12:42, 45-6, each quote a parable of Jesus in which a ruler departs into a far country. In Mt, the ruler leaves others in charge

A very important aspect of conscience is a person's sensitivity to goodness and justice. We cannot hope to throw up a proof of right and wrong action that will convince everybody, as we might count out a handful of coins on a table. Rather, right and wrong are learned, not only with our earliest learning but also in the harder school of experience that most of us live to encounter. Learning goodness is the work of a lifetime. The more immediate solution, however, to many moral problems is often suggested by expediency. Doing what is right often goes against the grain of ambitions that seem to lie deeper in the personality. One of the great themes of moral science is to seek some understanding of that counter appeal of goodness and personal cost.

In the scriptures of the Old Testament, the prophets looked forward not only to some coming deliverance of the people, but particularly it was a deliverance of the just and the poor. Prophecy attempted to name not just the future, but the truth of the present moment was named as well. Throughout the Bible we read frequently of the person who has the right to enter the tent of God, or to live on his holy mountain:

The man whose way of life is blameless,
who always does what is right,
who speaks the truth from his heart,
whose tongue is not used for slander,

Who does no wrong to his fellow,
casts no discredit on his neighbour'
looks with contempt upon the reprobate,
but honours those who fear Yahweh;

Who stands by his pledge at any cost,
Does not ask interest on loans,

---

of talents dues on which will be later collected, and in Lk the ruler sends a deputy and finally his own son in order to secure the inheritance from wicked men. See also Newman's *Sermons of the Day*, London 1843, XV1, where mention is made of these two texts: the concern here is to state that the apostles of Jesus, and their successors, are his delegates on earth; they are invested with the same authority and power as was his.

And cannot be bribed to victimise the innocent,
– If a man does all this, nothing can ever shake him.[6]

What we have here is an emphasis on the moral character of each person. The development of the moral character is an essential part of the faculty of conscience whether in the religious believer or in the non-believer. This should remind the believer of two general truths. Firstly, the providence of God was reaching out always to all of his creatures, even before a complete revelation of his own nature began to be communicated. Secondly, every person has some capacity for moral development.

The moral character of a person suggests, moreover, that there is a pre-disposition to recognise what is good and to distinguish this from what is evil. 'Pre-dispositions', 'hidden notices', 'prejudices', are often in favour of the good. Religion rests on these evidences as much as it rests on what can be seen and proved to the rational mind.[7]

The problem of evil

Inevitably, in talking about morals, the question of evil comes up. This is how Suzanne explained it:

Evil … I think evil is the loss of the norms. It is the loss, the absence of that motor that keeps us all going on the straight and narrow. At some level there is evil that is in us, which is where people have clinically lost their judgement … lost their ability to make decisions. Or they shift from the normal set of values, and that could be for clinical and medical reasons, or it could be the people who just keep slipping. Maybe these are the ones who test the boundaries and get away with it and move on. Think about criminology, you know, the kids from the areas where they are more exposed to crime etc. have different norms, so they are going to get more involved in it. So you will always have people at the edge, whose norms are different.

6. Ps 15:2-5. It need scarcely be pointed out that in a agrarian society such as existed in the ancient world, the moral issue of asking a neighbour for interest on a loan was a different one from that which exists in our world of commercial banking.
7. See Newman, *University Sermons*, (1843), Sermon II, 'The influence of natural and revealed religion respectively', London 1909, pp 16-36.

I asked her whether she ever felt herself to be tempted by evil, or in contact with evil, or had she any sense that there might be evil in herself:

No, I don't think I have personally come across anything that I would call evil. I would have often come across people who would have shifted their boundaries. That might be in the work place where people are cold and hard, and will sacrifice other people's feelings for themselves. Or it might be in the case of a murder, where somebody has lost the boundaries for whatever reason. It could be a gradual shift of their norms, or it could be a 'one off'. But in the sense of somebody being absolutely evil ... I don't know.

'Do you believe in personal sin?'

Well sin ... I would see the church and religion as sets of rules and social norms, and sin is when you deviate, when you go against it. That relies on social norms always ... being right if you like. And yet when you go to Nazism or whatever, that's when the rules shifted ... people were complying with the rules. I think evil is used to describe ... sometimes people who are just very ill.

Declan and I touched briefly on the problem of evil. It was in the context of the imagination and the scope of the imagination both to inspire and to deceive:

I think there is right and wrong ... there are things you do and there are things you don't do. I think it's a huge responsibility. I think that what distinguishes the human probably from the rest of creation, in so far as I know ... is we have our intellect, and everything, and we have imagination ... I think imagination is the biggest curse that we have and the greatest blessing that we have. Imagination is wonderful ... and can lead us into all kinds of interesting places and good places. It can lead us into the most evil places.

Theoretically speaking, the concept of evil is largely a religious one. Martin was very certain that evil had a spiritual source outside of man and woman. I began by asking him how important morals were to his belief:

Hugely important ... the moral code is contained in the Ten Commandments. But it is something else ... I mean there's an ethical concept, which goes along with that moral code and the recognition of the occasions when the code has been broken and people are going past the limits. How do you know that? I don't know how you know it but there are people who know it. You recognise that you are now exceeding the limit, or the ethical limits, where you shouldn't go, and where you are now engaged in breaking a moral code, and the moral code is extraordinarily strict ... it's almost humanly impossible ... it's almost humanly impossible to observe. That's why I come back to St Thérèse's attitude, when she couldn't deal with temptation, what did she do? She fled from it; she didn't stop to fight it, she just fled. Now you can say that's a coward's way out. But there are some things that are better to flee than to run the risk of becoming involved in a situation that you can't handle. That's very difficult; it's terribly difficult, in fact. You go through life aware of the proximity of moral danger, it's everywhere around us, it's constant.

Unfortunately we are now in a situation where the idea of a moral boundary ... there is no boundary anymore. An extraordinary thing I suppose is that there is still some kind of limitation out there, but when you read now all of these paedophile activities and the seductions and the destruction of young peoples' lives, you wonder how could human beings do these things to one another.

If there is no evil then it doesn't matter. If there is no satanic influence operating in the world, then this is just a development of some phase of human nature which we weren't conscious of before. But the more Satan intrudes in the world and obtains more influence, the more dangerous our lives become, and the more dangerous society and civilisation becomes. I am convinced that the only thing that prevents the balance between good and evil tipping over is the existence of the contemplative houses of prayer in various parts of the world.

'This is in God's hands ...', I commented. Martin continued:
You see the one thing I cannot understand is, and there hasn't been a great deal written about it, why did God give so much power to Satan? Satan's power is almost limitless; it is vast. And yet God gave him this vast power to corrupt and destroy very good-living human beings, none of whom can remotely approach the intelli-

gence of this evil influence. That's why one must constantly pray not only for oneself ... he's a very dangerous enemy, and he's much closer than people realise.

'Do you find that you are holding on by your fingertips when it comes to believing in Satan?'
No. No, I know that's real. I know that's real.

'Tell me how you know that that's real.'
I can't ... I don't know. I've felt it on many occasions. I've felt it on many occasions.

'You find it easier to believe in the evil than in the good ...'
No. I don't. I don't find it easier, except that I feel the evil is almost as much a reality as the good ... and it's because, because the reality of evil is so very close, because nobody recognises it, that it is so very dangerous ... I often think it's a pity that more and more attention isn't paid to the existence of this evil influence in the world. And again, you see: What proof do we have of the existence of God? And equally, what proof have we of the existence of Satan, except that, particularly in the last twenty, thirty, years the amount of depravity in the world and the amount of suffering caused to human beings by their fellow human beings has been of such a nature that no human being could possibly be so evil as to inflict that kind of suffering on somebody else.

In Northern Ireland, for the last twenty, twenty-five, years you have seen suffering of a kind inflicted on innocent people, such as the bombing of twelve, fourteen, twenty people ... no human ... over those years I would ask somebody: 'Could you imagine yourself shooting somebody in the leg, shooting somebody in the hand?' The response would always be: 'No.' Well then, can you imagine yourself blowing up that person's leg, blowing up that person's hand ... you shudder from the thought of it ... and yet there are people who are prepared to engage in this kind of thing without a second thought.

Paula is equally sure of the existence of evil in some personal form that is outside of humanity. I asked her for her general impression of what Satan was, or the devil, or evil ...

Evil ... I believe there is evil there ... there are evil people ... I mean,
I don't want the devil to come to me ... I don't like thinking of him,
I don't like talking of him, I would rather keep him as far away ...
but I believe there is evil out there in the world. I mean people mur-
der people ... mutilate people ... I mean there has to be ... then there
is all this 'Satanism'. And we would have friends that are pagans,
they are witches, you know the 'white witches' ... but I mean they
don't ... they are not into the dark side ... they would be into the
earth, the moon ...

'But you believe there is a dark side?' I asked.
Yes, definitely ... There was a thing on the television there two
weeks ago about a girl and a fellow in Germany ... drinking the
blood ... they were into Satanism. I can't ... I can't understand ...
my feelings again ... I mean I can't understand how people can feel
good about things like that. I mean, it must be horrible to have a be-
lief like that ... in the devil, where no good, where it's all no good.
Well from what I have learned from films I've seen and all the rest,
and books I've read, so ... yes, he is there. But I just don't know
anything about him ... I don't even like to talk about him.

The concept of evil presents itself in life. It concerns certain
bad behaviours, it has a religious dimension and it is strongly
imaginative.

Imagination and making sense
Let us look briefly at what is involved in the imaginative dimension of the mind. When Jesus told the parable about the good
Samaritan, the man who crossed the road to help the victim of
bandits and who brought him to an inn and paid for him there,
he was making a direct appeal to the imaginations of his listeners.[8] According to the story, several others, including some
priests, had passed by the dying man on the other side of the
road and had continued their journey. Jesus intended that people would identify themselves with the Samaritan, the outsider,
the one who was despised in that culture, and that they would

---

8. Lk 10:29-37.

recognise that it was he who was the true neighbour to the dying man. That is why the outsider in the story, the despised one, is called 'the good Samaritan'. All of the parables of Jesus appeal to the imagination; many of them present us with mental pictures of the world as it could be, not as it is. These pictures are ones that demand a choice, in this case a choice that would recognise the goodness of those who are different from us culturally.

It is because of our imagination that we associate God with notions of warmth, welcome, comfort, and hospitality. God is also associated with justice, firmness, correction and even punishment. We fill out our picture with impressions that come from the gospels. The content of our view of God can vary very much with the personal perspective and the moral character of the individual. If our perception corresponds with the perceptions of the gospels, we can believe then that they will be broadly true.

To take a very different example of the scope of the imagination, we can appeal to the science of physics. The black hole theory of collapsing stars in the universe is, at this time, a work of the scientific imagination.[9] The imagination comes to the aid of our intelligence and provides it with pictures and impressions of what cannot be seen directly. Imagination makes it possible for the intellect to make the jump from the senses to faith.

Our pictures of heaven are largely the work of imagination, as are the pictures of hell. A person, in the late Middle Ages, who contributed much to the imaginative understanding of the other world is the poet Dante. His poem 'The Divine Comedy' gives detailed impressions of what he imagines awaits us after death. Some of the popes and bishops who were alive in his lifetime are to be found in the depths of his hell. Yet, his vision of purgatory is an optimistic one that reaches towards heaven. In Dante's heaven, he meets again Beatrice, a girl whom he idealised and loved since his youth.

But imagination doesn't necessarily lead to God. 'Imagine

---

9. See *Black Holes* by Isaac Asimov, in *The Faber Book of Science*, ed. John Carey, London 1995, pp 421-22.

there's no heaven', sang John Lennon, 'it's easy if you try.'[10] Imagination is the seat of our own individual creativity, and such is the way that it works, we can imagine anything that we wish. 'It's easy if you try.' We can screen out everything that has to do with support and well being, if we wish. We can create a world of make believe and of self delusion too, just for the fun of it. The world that each of us inhabits is to a greater extent than is usually realised a world that is created by our own minds. Imagination is defined as the 'mental faculty of forming images of objects not present; fancy; creative faculty of the mind'.[11]

John Lennon and Dante stand at the opposite ends of a spectrum of imagination. John says: imagine that there is nothing supernatural, 'no God and no religion too'. He sees around him a world of religious and ethnic conflict, and imagines that he will save it by purging it of all belief. This is his way to peace. Dante says: imagine everything that you can, everything that is permitted within the bounds of Christian doctrine and belief. Dante sees the ideals of Christ, the world as it has been created by God and abused by human beings. He invents a whole schematic and pictorial view of the future life, so as to alert his contemporaries to the full reality of what is going on in their lives now, and to what awaits them when they die. Speaking of God, Beatrice tells the poet, 'In His will is found our peace'.[12] Lennon and Dante are alike in that they offer us the reflection of their imaginations. Like them, we too must imagine.

Another famous work of the imagination is the poem 'The Dream of Gerontius' by John Henry Newman.[13] The dream tells the story of an old man who approaches death and who is filled with hope and also with dread at the prospect of meeting God. As the verses progress and the old man dies, the story moves to the other side of the grave where we find him gathered up by his guardian angel and transported to the throne of God. Whether

10. A well-known pop song of the 1970s by John Lennon.
11. *Oxford Pocket Dictionary*, op. cit., p 392.
12. *The Divine Comedy*, III, *Il Paradiso*, 3. 85.
13. See *Verses on Various Occasions*, London, 1868.

in reference to this life or to the next, every detail of the poem reflects this world as we see it and as we feel it now. Newman uses fully the pictures that we have through faith and expands this imaginatively to create a picture that is both credible and moving. Edward Elgar set the work to music. The reader of the poem or the listener to the music retains a great sense of the peace that is expected to follow upon a happy death.

In a very real sense, our world chooses us. Words like 'realistic', 'believable', 'unbelievable' are adjectives that colour basic values. There is a world of moral relativity and there is a world in which ultimate values do exist. There is a world in which there is no supernatural dimension, nothing beyond the visible and tangible, nothing other than the actual here and now. And there is a world that intersects with spiritual values, wider realities, however we may sketch them. We assent to our values because they appeal to us, they impress us. We are carried to our decisions by many things on the way that have fallen into place for us.

CHAPTER FOUR

Discovering General Knowledge

Most of us make our way through life without thinking too much about how the human mind works. We tend not to engage in serious reflection on the subject of our own knowledge. Like the engine under the bonnet of a car, the fact that it works is usually good enough. We move from thought A to thought B with relative ease. In what follows, I would like to lift 'the bonnet' of the mind and examine more closely some aspects of what is to be observed there.

We know from Declan how he picked up his early learning in the home and at school:

I was told where creation had come from, who it had come from, what our part was in it, how we were to behave in it ... what would happen us if we didn't behave. It was all very structured, in a way very simple ... and it never occurred to me to actually question, it seemed self- evident, there must be some purpose for our being here ... and where did we go from here, which was another basic question. There were very simple answers to that, they were available in school, they were available in the ordinary culture of that time.

And yet, as we know, on leaving the home environment as a young man, this whole scenario fell apart for him.

My main argument is in two parts: first, to show that general knowledge is a knowing of persons, facts and values. General knowledge depends on our own picking up of the facts and clues that are all about us; it follows from the interaction that takes place between us and the environment. I then want to show that religious knowledge, in this sense, is like all knowledge. It is unlike other knowledge, however, in that its ultimate origins lie in God's own revelation of 'himself' to humankind.

Religious knowledge depends completely on the gracious act of a giving God. In the act of faith, these two, general knowledge and religious knowledge, are deeply intertwined. With a little effort, however, we can almost separate them and examine each one in turn. But they belong together, even as we look at them separately. We begin by examining general knowledge in this chapter; we will look at religious knowledge in the next.

See, Judge, Act

All knowledge is about life and action. There is no such thing as pure knowledge in the sense that it is unrelated to our experience and to our humanity. We are not 'intellects' simply; we are always human beings in the world. With this in mind, let us try to understand how we know a simple fact to be the case. Perhaps the best way of coming to understand the way the mind works is to think of it in terms of the well-known triad: See, Judge and Act.[1]

'See' refers to our perception of reality. That is, we look at or examine something in order to discover what it is. Or it may be that we listen to something, or that we taste it, or simply that we touch it. At all events, we take it in with our senses. Perception comes by way of the senses. But more than our senses are involved in perception. In order to see what we see, or to hear what we hear, we draw upon knowledge that we have already acquired. What we have already come to know plays an essential role in understanding or knowing what it is that we perceive now. There is no such thing as 'direct' perception without foreknowledge. A blind person cannot hope to recognise what is visible simply by having 'physical' sight given to him. He has to learn to comprehend, to understand what he sees. Perception is always a function of what we encounter through our senses and, at the same time, a function of what we already know.

---

1. This triad is not dissimilar from the ancient 'Thought , Word and Deed', that is found as early as St Gregory of Nyssa, c 334-394, *On Christian Perfection*, J. P. Migne, *Patrologia Graeca* 46. 283, quoted in *The Divine Office*, Week 12, Tuesday, p 224, vol 3.

'Judge' refers to the personal or individual component in the act of knowing. It is the active as opposed to the passive aspect in coming to know. In other words, in addition to perception, the individual person needs to make a judgement about the reality that is before him or her. A character in Shakespeare's *Macbeth* asks: 'Is this a dagger I see before me?'[2] Is it the case that this is really so? Through the personal act of judgement that follows this implicit question, each of us appropriates ordinary reality. Without this act of judgement, there would be no significant difference between our dreaming states and our waking states.

If we stay with this 'judge' moment, something further becomes apparent to us. Our personal judgement actually goes beyond a mere apprehension of facts. What we find is that 'we know that we know'. That is, our capability of judgement flows also from the build-up of knowledge that has accumulated over time. So the 'judge' moment, as well as the 'see' moment, is accompanied by previously acquired knowledge. The gradual accumulation of knowledge, in other words, brings with it what we might call a 'recognition' factor that facilitates new judgements.

This sense of 'I know that I know' is a kind of reflexive awareness on the part of the knower. It is difficult to explain it further. We know something to be the case not simply because someone has told us so, but also because our own assent to the fact confirms it in some way. We are now more certain of the matter, despite other views to the contrary. When we reflect on it, we realise that the kind of knowledge whereby we know that as human beings we are free, or whereby we know that in some basic sense we are all equal, emanates from this reflexive aspect of human judgement. This is the kind of knowledge on which we might take a stand at the cost of our comfort, or our jobs or

---

2. *Macbeth*, Act 2, scene 1: In this case Macbeth finds himself torn between the truth value of an apparition of a bloodied dagger before his eyes, and his own less than determined intention to commit the murder that shortly follows. He is making a complex judgement about his own perception.

even our lives. Like the mathematical fact that the whole is greater than the part, this kind of knowledge has a self-evidence about it that is utterly convincing. Yet, unlike the example of the whole and the part, a more precise delineation of this self-evidence often eludes us.

And now let us look at the 'Act' part of the triad. Imagine that we are on a sea voyage, and that it is night. The course has been plotted according to our latest positions, insofar as these were known accurately. Imagine now that ahead of us in the darkness we see an intermittent bright light. From what we had already known, let us suppose we have been expecting a lighthouse at about this time. So, we gladly identify the light and maintain or adjust or alter our course accordingly. Another way of thinking of the act is that it is a knowing 'how', as opposed to a knowing 'that'. This mental adjustment or alteration completes the act of knowing. It is the 'act'.

On reflection, it will appear that all of what we know and do can be understood as having been formed and executed in the manner that the model suggests. We can recognise now the role played by knowledge that we already have, both in our own perceptions, and in our judgement of them, and in our action upon them.

Some facts about knowledge
Most of what we know is, in fact, accepted on the testimony of others.[3] It is based on information we have received from them, or on their knowledge and work, as the navigator's knowledge is based on what is to be read in the coastal charts. Although I

3. For a relatively accessible overall guide to understanding knowledge, see Michael Polanyi, *Personal Knowledge: towards a post critical philosophy*, London 1958 (paperback 1973). What follows is a thumbnail sketch of what 'knowledge' is. The words and the concepts used are largely my own. A person tends to describe a familiar landscape in terms that are of his choosing. In *Grammar of Assent*, op. cit., we read: '*Everyone who thinks on these subjects takes a course of his own, though it will also happen to be the course which others take besides himself ... I gave notice just now that I should offer my own witness in the matter in question; though of course it would not be worthwhile my offering it, unless what I felt myself agreed with*

have never seen Siberia, I have seen what purport to be photographs of the place, and I accept without any demur the fact that it exists. I assume that it is there.

Our moral values are also learned from others. The value of 'fairness' is one that was taught to me, but very quickly I came to accept it as being true for its own sake, even though I may not have reflected on it. So it is that 'valuing things' quickly becomes a kind of hidden capability. It is there without our being aware that it is there. Such assumed and hidden knowledge and capability forms our information base and it informs and determines our perspectives on the world and on our actions in the world.

This process is continuous. It starts at the beginning of life and, as we grow older, we appropriate perspectives, values, mind-sets, which make up the frame through which we view and interpret experience. For the most part, we accept, initially at any rate, what is accepted by those with whom we live. Even if we have rebelled and thrown over the values of our parents, whether for a time or for good, the new values tend to be ones that are accepted by the 'circle' in which we *now* live. We appropriate and make our own those values that in our own view serve us best.

For the great majority of us, our investigation of what we know is not rigorous. We take our knowledge on the word of others. This knowledge includes all of those certainties of the modern worldview that have come to be accepted by our age. When someone speaks about the speed of light, for example, it is accepted as part of the normal currency of knowledge that light travels and that its speed can be computed. Very few would have more than a rudimentary awareness of these matters or of how recently they became common knowledge. Or when a person speaks about holding property, or buying a house, it is assumed that private ownership is a value that can be justified without further question.

---

what is felt by hundreds and thousands besides me, as I am sure it does, whatever be the measure, more or less, of their explicit recognition of it.' Op. cit., p 318. Here Newman is writing of Revealed Religion, but his remarks apply equally as well in my context.

The enormous range of 'assumed' knowledge, moreover, does not suggest a strange or unusual state of affairs. The ordinary business of daily life everywhere depends on it. The greatest intellects known to us have had to take much of what was reality for them on the word of others. And knowledge of things in the real world as well as knowledge of things in the human imagination, fables and stories and the like, is stored and used by us with an awareness of the significance that these kinds of knowledge offers.

During the course of our lives we may also acquire knowledge that is more than assumed knowledge. Knowledge that goes with acquiring a skill, or a trade, or a profession, is this kind of knowledge. Such an 'acquired' knowledge comes from a more diligent inquiry or apprenticeship into something whether for the sake of knowing it or for the sake of making a living from it. A seasoned navigator is a person who has obtained over years the knowledge, skill and experience whereby he or she has mastered the hazards of living at sea. Acquired knowledge is knowledge that is hard won; it comes with practice and with perseverance. That is one reason why some people are so much more knowledgeable and more skilled than others. It may happen also that the knowledge that comes from mistakes or from reversals in fortune is this type of knowledge rather than knowledge that is simply assumed or automatically learned. It is why we say that wisdom is something that comes with age. Each of these kinds of knowledge, moreover, belongs to the natural range of human knowing.

I have consciously chosen to describe knowledge in terms of assumed and acquired because these terms suggest exactly what we need to understand about knowledge at this stage.[4] In fact, as we grow older, the need to acquire knowledge may lessen, and

4. The distinction between 'assumed' and 'acquired' knowledge was a favourite one of Newman; see *Grammar of Assent*, op. cit., ch 3, pp 33ff. In his *Idea of a University*, delivered originally as a series of lectures in Dublin in 1852, Newman lays out his understanding of knowledge: '*All that exists, as contemplated by the human mind, forms one large system or complex fact, and this of course resolves itself into an indefinite number of*

the taking in of assumed knowledge may increase, because the actual pathways of knowledge have become so much more developed in the person. The formation of intuition may well be related to this development.

There are many different kinds and degrees of assumed and acquired knowledge. There is what might be called factually based knowledge that has a large component of information, and there is value based knowledge where the requirement of judgement is particularly important. On the factual side, we can think of the sciences and mathematics whereas, on the value or appreciative side, we can think of morals, music or the arts. The whole spectrum of knowledge is very wide. It includes every aspect of every subject known to us, from calculation to evaluation, from language to literature.

To speak about assumed or learned knowledge at this level, we must examine more closely the world of the intellect which makes all and any knowledge possible. The intellect is a power in the human being that admits to levels of knowledge and culture that appear to transcend the sensory and material environment in which these levels of knowledge are mediated. It is not unlike the electric current that passes through a wire. The current and the wire, while being compatible, are also very different from each other.

The universe and all that it contains is physical and material as far as we can see. Yet our handling of ideas and values leads us to suppose that levels of meaning exist that are not material. It doesn't make sense to ask how big an idea is, no matter how big it may seem to us to be. Ideas and size do not match up. Nor does an idea have an age, in the usual sense, as everything material has. An immediate response to this might be to say that ideas cannot exist but, within a short time, we would realise the absurdity of such a proposition. This leads us to posit the exist-

---

particular facts, which, as being portions of a whole, have countless relations of every kind, one towards another. Knowledge is the apprehension of these facts, whether in themselves, or in their mutual positions and bearings.' 2, p 45, London, 1919. In these two sentences he has summarised the work of a university and of all the faculties within it.

ence of some kind of universal domain, let us call it the intellectual domain, which exists in some manner that is different from the way in which matter as we know it exists. This intellectual domain appears to be of a different order from material reality. It alone can put us in touch with reality, and it alone can enable us to make judgements about that reality. It is with this largely unnoticed 'intellectual' dimension of all knowledge that we must reckon.

Knowledge and belief

Central to this hidden intellectual dimension of knowledge is a kind of trust or basic belief. This is the case whether the knowledge in question is personal knowledge, or factual, or any other kind. Knowledge is always based on a kind of prior belief. Belief seems to be embedded in the nature of knowledge and in the reality of language. To understand a word, or its underlying concept, you have to believe that you are in touch somehow with that which is being spoken of. This primitive act of intellectual belief may be overlooked in many accounts of the act of knowing, accounts that assume that the mind reads directly from the book of nature without any affirmative intervention or participation from the reader.

The phrase 'I believe that I may understand' goes to the heart of my argument.[5] Belief or trust, in this sense, is part of that framework, that worldview that is presupposed, when any act

5. This phrase *'Credo ut intelligam'* was first used by Anselm (1033-1109) in respect of the revealed word of God, a much narrower meaning than the one that I intend here. An account of his thought is found in Frederic Copleston SJ, *A History Of Philosophy*, Vol 2, Augustine to Scotus, (London 1959) XIV, pp 156-165. Polanyi shows that the idea of a personal warrant for belief is present in every assertion of truth; see *Personal Knowledge*, op. cit. pp 252-257, 279-286, 299ff. The same idea is found in Newman's thought: *'Nothing, then, which Scripture says about Faith, however startling it may be at first sight, is inconsistent with the state in which we find ourselves by nature with reference to the acquisition of knowledge generally, a state in which we must assume something to prove anything, and can gain nothing without a venture.'* University Sermons 1843, Sermon XI 'The Nature of Faith In Relation To Reason', pp 214-5.

of knowing takes place. Unless I believe that something is capable of being understood, that it can be understood within the frame of reference of my own knowing, then I cannot hope to understand it. So belief is always necessary, in that it precedes understanding and it precedes knowledge.

Seeing and believing are very different intellectual activities obviously. One is based on perception; the other is based on trusting what one has already learned. What is not so readily recognised is that there is no perception at all unless there is a very particular kind of trust associated with it. At sea, a flashing light in the darkness could mean anything, but the fact that we know about lighthouses and that we are expecting to see one at about this time is what informs our perception of the light.

From earliest days, we have been taught to recognise what we see. This primitive naming of everything continues in ever more sophisticated spirals as we grow up. Those who help us in our recognising and naming of things are our parents, our brothers and sisters, friends and teachers, and perhaps role models we have chosen. The naming applies to objects, feelings, values, persons and ideas. When something occurs within our field of vision, or our hearing, or other senses, and when we recognise what it is, only then can we begin to say that we know it.

As well as providing new knowledge, however, this naming process can be abused. Abuse occurs when people are fraudulently shown something as if it was something else or they are led to believe something to be a fact that is not a fact. Counterfeit money is an example of such abuse. It thrives because of deception. People think that it is the real thing and it is not.

If something appears that has never been encountered before, or is not explained to us in some way, then we are confused. The distress that is suffered with the onset of illness is an example of this. The confusion is removed when the new experience is named. Have we not heard people say: 'It is a serious illness, but I am happier because now I have some idea of what is wrong with me'?

Science today

Among the most important aspects of general knowledge in our world today are those that concern the facts and values of science. Science is a unique method of looking at reality and of studying it closely. In its own turn, the scientific method needs to be carefully considered and evaluated. The scientific method is another way of gathering knowledge.

Scientific knowledge, like other knowledge, has an objective and a subjective dimension. The notion that science alone is totally objective cannot be sustained. This dependence of science on the judgement of the scientist has been shown particularly by the nature of reality itself as it has come to be seen in the twentieth century.[6]

Science is built on experiments. The scientific method runs like this: preconceptions must be treated as suspect until such time as they are shown scientifically to be the case. In order to verify a hypothesis, it must first be assumed that the hypothesis is not the case, even though one may anticipate it to be so. That is, the matter to be verified is 'hypothesised'. This is so that an experiment can be designed which will show it to be the case. Then, if the experiment is successful, the hypothesis is shown, provisionally at any rate, to be the true one. If the experiment does not underwrite the hypothesis, then one has to begin again with a new and different experiment, or a new hypothesis.

Through this work or process, the naming or hypothesising of new theories is at the front line of scientific discovery. Science produces new knowledge, and this new knowledge is then incorporated into our daily assumptions, usually without further interrogation. If we look for a moment at the work being done in medical research, we can see this process quite clearly. In seeking a cure for cancer, research focuses imaginatively on new approaches that might have a better effect than those in use at the present time. These approaches are examined for their suitability

6. See F. W. Bridgeman and others 'Uncertainty and Other Worlds', and Max Born 'Quantum Mechanics: Mines and Machine Guns', in *The Faber Book of Science*, ed. John Carey, London 1995, pp 277-285. See also Polanyi, op. cit., (*Objectivity and Modern Physics*) pp 15-17.

at many different levels, and they are tested on animals and then on willing patients. If all goes well, and if it can be shown that the new treatment offers real benefits that no existing treatment can offer, and that it has no detrimental side effects, or side effects that are acceptable relative to a good outcome, then the treatment becomes more generally available and takes its place alongside other successful treatments or replaces them.

However, some of the conditions for verification that are deliberately specified by science have tended to become general assumptions that are unconsciously held by people generally. It is assumed, for example, that all of the conclusions of popular science have been rigorously tested. This is not so. Popular perceptions of the scientific method sometimes suggest that because science or technology says so then the question is closed. Yet the average person is usually well aware of how today's scientific certainty, in the matter of foods, to take just one example, becomes tomorrow's casualty.[7]

Science exists at the rational level of human judgement, a level that can be overturned by a new 'reason' not yet discovered. However, this new knowledge, valuable as it is, tells us nothing about those more ultimate issues that have to do with our common humanity. As persons we must find ways of relating to each other that reflect properly our human nature. But it is outside the province of science to tell us about humanity at this level. It is a judgement that we make on different grounds, not scientific ones. Many of the basic attitudes that give shape to our values tend to come, for the most part, from our judgements about these more ultimate issues.

---

7. In other ways, people tend to forget what science tells us and they cling to their original 'common sense' perceptions of things. We are told, for example, that nothing is solid because everything at the micro level is composed of atoms that are for the most part empty space. Probably most of us still speak of a sun that rises and sets everyday, some five centuries since Galileo showed that it was the rotation of the earth that created this impression.

Science and religious faith

This brings us to the relationship and the important distinctions that exist between science and religious faith. Faith is above rationality somehow, yet consistent with it. When we reflect on it, we notice for example that the recognition of human dignity or the 'uniqueness' of human beings is something that lies outside the strict parameters of experimental science. This difference of emphasis needs to be clearly understood in order to clear the way for an appreciation of religious faith.

The 'scientific method' is itself a powerful and persuasive interpretation of reality. Yet it may pose a threat to belief in God even if, in the view of scholars, including scholars of science, it is a false threat. Unless it can be proven that God exists, the argument goes, then 'God' is suspect. Because it is not possible, however, to show by any experimental method that God exists, many draw a false conclusion that there is no reason to believe that God is there.

Apart from so-called 'new age' movements, this consensus of received knowledge tends to reject that which cannot be explained or shown to be true in a 'scientific' way. But God cannot be proven in the way that an experiment is proven. It was Aristotle who said: 'It is the mark of an educated man not to demand more proof than a subject admits of.'[8] Yet we live in an age that tends to take for granted the impression that everything that can be seen and touched, whether by hand or with the aid of an instrument, is there, but nothing else is. A microscope, for example, cannot measure the values by which we live.

There is a further caution to be noted. Much of the ordinary world that we perceive in and through our culture, we see through a kind of positive filter. We often tend to see the beauty of the world rather than the struggle for survival, whether in the human or in the animal kingdoms. This, in association with other causes, is because our vision of everything is already impregnated with many of the colours and the values of the Judeo-Christian heritage. If we strip this vision away, and look simply

8. Aristotle (384-322 BC), *Nichomachean Ethics*, 1. 3.

at the mere evidence for God as it presents itself, as scientists do when they observe phenomena, the way to God may seem a lot less certain. Arguably, up until the present age, many believers held that the natural evidence of the world supplied them with an explanation of God. In ancient times, various natural phenomena were understood to be 'acts of God' in a very real sense. For many people today, science has removed this possibility and so this 'naked' world without God has become a very cold place.[9]

The rise of technology and science has been accompanied in many countries by a context of religious decline. It is true, of course, that religious truth has never been a top priority in the daily world of human affairs. For the most part, places of public meeting and exchange are not exercised with the truths of religion for their own sake and never have been. Yet, in the world of modern technological and scientific culture, it seems increasingly that many of the questions connected with God have simply dropped away. The question 'what happens us when we die', for example, does not seem to present itself with the same force to the human mind as was once the case. Questions like this are frequently assumed to be part of the baggage of a bygone age, but they are universal questions about ultimate issues to do with our humanity.

Metaphor and Analogy
When we examine knowledge, we see that it can be direct or it can be indirect. Direct knowledge is when we know something that we can see and verify for ourselves, even if we have learned it from someone else. Indirect knowledge is when we know something that is at some remove from our everyday experi-

9. Yet, here too, it is possible to take a false path. It could be said that what is really needed in the world is a proper sense of materiality. The status of many desirable objects in the consumer society relates not so much to the things themselves as to the sense of need for them that is created by pressures such as advertising. So it is the status that having this car confers, or that house, that is important, rather than the car itself or the house. And so we live in an 'immaterial' world of values and pressures that is quite unrelated to the world of our real needs.

ence, yet we possess an explanation that makes it possible to know and understand it, whether wholly or partially.

We use metaphor when we use a colourful or a telling image that conveys the essence of something, even though the image properly belongs to something else. When Homer spoke of the 'rosy handed' dawn,[10] he was drawing attention to something that we would all instantly recognise. Yet few of us could describe it so accurately. Metaphor shows us another way in which we lay hold of reality that is somewhat at a distance from us, or more complex or difficult to express. Metaphor is used constantly in every sphere of knowledge, not just religious knowledge. It extends the field of knowledge and of expression. It points towards that which cannot be expressed in any other or better way.

We use analogy when we make a comparison of one thing with another, even though there is an unlikeness between them that we momentarily overlook in order to make the comparison. When we say, for example, that the man and the plant are both alive, it could be said that we are using the word 'alive' analogically. Although alive means the same thing in both instances, yet the instances themselves are sufficiently diverse to suggest that the alive might be quite different in each case. Analogy makes it possible to take over, as it were, whole aspects of reality that are otherwise quite inaccessible to us. It is an ordinary intellectual facility that tends very much to be taken for granted.[11]

Much of our knowing is by way of analogy. We can see the importance of it when we consider some of the concepts that are used every day in science. We hear of the 'law of gravity', for example, and yet a little reflection shows that gravity cannot be a law in any ordinary sense of the meaning of that word. There is no 'law' in space. The term is used analogically to convey ideas of 'governance', 'obedience' and 'certainty' in the planetary domain. An aspect of human life with which we are familiar is

10. *The Iliad*, Harmondsworth, 1950, tr E. V. Rieu, Bk 1, p 35. According to Rieu, Homer lived in the 10th century BC.
11. *Metaphor and Religious Language*, by Janet Martin Soskice, Oxford 1985, is a very helpful guide.

projected onto the dynamic relationship between objects in space. We are so used to these ways of speaking that we hardly notice them.

The use of analogy shows, furthermore, that to understand what is meant by knowledge, whether in science or law or religion or in any subject, we need to penetrate beyond the actual field of the knowledge in question. We do this whenever we 'know' something because we penetrate, without realising it, to a level that distinguishes knowledge from mere information, as for example when we distinguish between knowledge of what is real and fantasy knowledge. We penetrate to this level whenever we know something that is not immediately obvious to the perception of the senses.

Metaphor and analogy are forms of linguistic expression and of intellectual comprehension that extend the scope of the human mind. They point to things or to states of affairs in the real world, and they describe them indirectly. They find ways of identifying something by comparing it with that which is more familiar and more 'to hand'. They are examples of the way that we can acquire indirect knowledge. The uses of metaphor and analogy bring us further along the road of understanding and they show us different ways in which knowledge throws light on reality.

It is important to state that not every metaphor or every analogy is a good one. There can be bad metaphors and false analogies that do not really or adequately convey the matter at issue.

Frequently, we use metaphor and analogy to speak of ideas about which we are only vaguely aware. Religion is the attempt to speak of that domain beyond the present moment of which we have no direct knowledge. And so, for example, we speak of 'garden' as a metaphor for creation, or of 'our father' as an analogy for God. When we use these terms in this sense, we speak of images from our own experience, but we use them in a unique way to extend our knowledge.

The poet Philip Larkin, who described himself as an atheist, is conscious of the value of metaphor when he writes of the beauty and wonder of the countryside in summer. In his poem 'Cut Grass',[12] he speaks of the 'Long, long death' of cut grass:

It dies in the white hours / Of young-leafed June
With chestnut flowers, / With hedges snowhite strewn,

White lilac bowed, / Lost lanes of Queen Anne's lace,
And that high-builded cloud / Moving at Summer's pace.

Larkin's use of metaphor extends somehow our understanding of this world in which we live by drawing the mind and imagination beyond the literal. I see the summer cloud but I also believe I see the meaning-laden quality of it that speaks to him and to me of its passing glory. An example of this kind of meaning-laden thinking is to be found in the book of Isaiah:

For as the earth brings forth its shoots,
And as a garden causes what is sown in it to spring up,
So the Lord God will cause righteousness and praise
to spring forth before all the nations.[13]

The contemporary believer knows exactly what the ancient author means. Just as the earth is there and the garden is there in all their vitality, so too, the believer knows, God is there telling us about his plan for the world. The analogy used by the author enables the mind to encompass that which can only be understood indirectly.

The distinction between direct experience and that which can only be experienced indirectly by way of metaphor or analogy brings us full circle, almost, in this discussion of religious knowledge. When we reflect on the wide range of things that are experienced only indirectly, we realise how normal it is to move though the world with only an indirect experience of much of what the world offers.

People of faith claim to be in touch with a domain in or beyond the present moment of which we have, of ourselves, no direct knowledge. For many people this domain is 'second nature'.

---

12. Philip Larkin, *Collected Poems*, London 1988, p 183.
13. Isaiah 61:11. This passage in Isaiah dates probably from some time around 540 BC.

It is as if they have a seamless overlay of the basic nature that all have received; an overlay of perception and of response that takes one into the worlds of faith and of prayer. For them it is a form not only of speech and thought but also of reality. These 'reflective' aspects of religious knowledge are the themes of our next chapter.

CHAPTER FIVE

Reflection and Religious Knowledge

The reflective element is an important aspect of all knowledge. In the case of religious knowledge in particular, that moment when one looks up from the printed page, or from whatever object that is being viewed, and simply allows the mind to wander or to rest in its own thought, is very precious. Religious knowledge is first and foremost a personal and subjective judgement on what presents to the mind. We need to sketch out the broad lines of such judgements. The content of this chapter may appear to be very tentative indeed to some readers. I would ask them to bear with this, with a view to a more definite picture later on.

Here, I want to set out, as simply as I can, the personal sources of religious knowledge. For the most part, I will examine what may be called 'natural' religion. By that is meant the religious awareness that is available to people simply by virtue of their being human. It might be an awareness that we would associate with someone who lives close to nature.

Our understanding of this world and of religion has to do with human knowledge. Hence the importance of sifting different elements that combine with one another in the act of knowing. It is through a particular appreciation of this world that we inhabit that we come upon matters that have to do with God.

If we look at some familiar concepts, such as justice, health, infinity and goodness, we can begin to see, through the use of metaphor and analogy, how these can take us into the realms of religious thought and of God.

All legal processes rest on the idea of justice. When we seek to define justice exactly, we are led to various illustrations of what we know it must mean: equity, fairness, doing right, avoiding wrongdoing, redress of wrong and so on. The question may be asked: is justice simply a generalisation of some kind, or an imaginative device perhaps? What do we mean when we say that justice demands such and such? Do we mean to say that justice, in any sense, actually exists? Is there anything really there, outside of the mind that is thinking it, that corresponds to the idea of justice? This reflection on something that certainly underpins law, or ought to, is not unlike the kind of reflection that is characteristic of faith.

The concept of health as it occurs in everyday usage presupposes a state of well-being that should exist in all living creatures and in all environments. I speak of a well-being that is physical and, in the case of humans, intellectual and emotional. It is a sense of well-being that we pursue and to which we willingly submit – to be in the whole of our health. Sometimes we may need to be shown this well-being, or taught to recognise it, when we are in danger of damaging our health because of our own behaviour. Belief in the concept of health can be an analogue for a wider and deeper belief. It can be a kind of underlying clue to the idea of religious wholeness, to a sense of purpose or intention in nature, and from there to another 'whole' being that has created the universe and that has created us in it.

The concept of infinity that we use when talking about outer space also has an analogy in religion. We speak of infinity in God. We have very little to go on when we formulate this concept in relation to God, yet we have sufficient to recognise that the meaning of infinity in God must be something like the meaning it has in space. It is something like what we find in God, in that it points to what appears to us as limitless; it contrasts with the word finite, meaning bounded and limited. Yet it is something unlike what is found in God in that it is quite beyond the scope of the intellect to understand infinity in God, at least as the intellect is presently constituted.

Finally, we come to the idea of goodness. Here is a quality that we are very familiar with and that we use every day. What exactly does it mean? The definition that is to be found in *The Pocket Oxford Dictionary* speaks of 'good' as an adjective, meaning: 'having the right qualities; adequate', and of 'goodness' as a noun, meaning: 'virtue, excellence, kindness'. These meanings, and some others, are spelled out over two columns of text.[1] We realise as Christians that some of the meaning of the word 'good' must also apply to God because, in his revelation to us, God is spoken of in just these terms. How goodness applies to God we cannot exactly know. We are only familiar with goodness insofar as it applies to realities that we are in touch with here on earth.

The study of analogy takes us to the borders of religious reflection. We have the concept of justice, and so we who believe in the Christian God believe that God must be just; we have the concept of health and wholeness, and we believe that God must be whole; we have the concept of infinity, and we believe that God must be infinite; we have the concept of goodness, and we recognise from what we have already been told that God is good. Having these concepts, of course, does not prevent us from committing the fallacy of shaping God simply according to our own view of him or her. Yet, the recognition that this can still happen may save us from such an outcome.

Some objections
To develop the view that there is a hidden God, it is necessary to show that some knowledge of God can be possible, however inadequate that knowledge may be. A position that held that any knowledge of God is inherently impossible, of its nature, would stall this argument at the very first step. Yet this is the very position that is taken up, admittedly in slightly different ways, by Declan and by Suzanne. For Declan, it is essential to human thought that we dismiss any idea of God, because any possible God is always irredeemably 'outside of' the field of human perception.

In my conversation with Declan, it was clear that the way

---

1. F. G. Fowler & H. W. Fowler, Reprinted edition 1967.

that he thinks about our knowledge of the universe contributes directly to his being an unbeliever in the religious sense:

Life is, in many ways, the only thing we have. It's obviously of such incredible value to us that you cannot think outside it. It's incredibly valuable to us ... not just us as individuals ... it is everything. It is every human, it is every animal, it is the insensate elements such as the rocks ... they are all part of it. So we are all part of this circle ... that is how I now like to think of it ... as a very large, very complex thing of which we are all absolutely made part ... and that other parts of life, in a way, we depend on, and other parts depend on us. So it's a very complex ... and when you stand back it's a very simple ... whole ... you have this infinitely interdependent, yes interdependent thing, of which we are part.

I asked him if it was his view that this phenomenon that we were all part of could only be understood from within:

I think we're trapped very much in language and structures, intellectual structures and mental structures. So we talk about 'out there'... but what do we mean by 'out there'? I'm not interested in 'out there'; I'm interested in 'in here'. And 'in here' is not 'me', 'ego', 'myself'... that kind of thing. I think 'in here' is the totality of our experience. And I begin to wonder whether we are not kidding ourselves, in fact, playing snakes and ladders with 'in here' and 'out there' ... and we are just using the wrong devices to address the issue. The ultimate reality is beyond all of this ... and its not some supernatural thing out there floating above the clouds. I think we have to get outside our 'normal' way of seeing things ... to grasp what 'reality' is, and then it may be inexpressible. So that the ultimate name of the new term ... whether you call it faith or belief or whatever ... it may be an experience of ... the 'is-ness' of being ... the fact that it 'is' at all. It hasn't really happened to me very often, but occasionally in the most mundane type of circumstance ... it has just come to me that 'that tree', for example ... is miraculous ... not because it is beautiful, which it may or may not be ... nor because I have grown it, nor because it is nicely positioned ... but because of the very fact that it's there. And if you try to express this ... you know, its 'being there', its 'is-ness' ... it is quite striking. I've not

been able to extend that ... probably I'd be totally overcome if I ex-
tended this to everything ... but I think somewhere 'in there' is what
might convince me that there is more than the superficiality of what
we live with and see everyday. But I don't think its a 'supernatural'
thing; I think it is the most 'natural thing' there is.

Suzanne also has a somewhat similar perception of an enclosed universe:

I think, as human beings we can't know anything around, outside
of our own experience, our own world ... so we imagine and we
make up what it might be ...

I asked her if she saw religion as a projection of some kind:

Well, I think it is a projection. It is a very handy projection, and it is
a very nice projection, but I find it particularly difficult to believe.

Suzanne is of the opinion that to believe in a God may simply
be an unconscious attempt to create something that does not
exist.

In order to hold open the possibility of belief, both Declan
and Suzanne's perspectives would have to be rejected as they
stand. It might seem at first that they have set down not unrea-
sonable limitations to what we can know as human beings.
From the point of view of the person who is open to religious belief, however, these limitations cannot be accepted. Both Declan
and Suzanne have presented what might be called an 'interior'
view of what is. Believers sense that they belong to a universe
that can be viewed 'exteriorly', even though such a view is available only to God.

To be open to religious belief is to reckon with the following
possibility: that we as human beings have already been communicated with by someone who exists completely outside of and
beyond our own environment, yet in a language that we can follow. This is the possibility that is envisaged by a 'revealed' religion. Furthermore, the believer takes heart from the ways in
which hidden realities may be explored indirectly as, for example, through metaphor and analogy.

On the concept of God

Let us begin our exploration of religious knowledge with the realisation that, if there is a God, then there can only be one God. That is, if there is some ultimate uncreated source of everything, then there can only be one such ultimate source. When we name that source as God, then a second God is impossible. Whatever other 'heavenly' beings may or may not exist, they are dependent on the One who is above and beyond all of creation.

A second realisation seems to follow from this. It is that God, if 'he' exists, must have already existed from all eternity. It may be possible to imagine an author of everything who, from the first moment in time, began to exist. Such a being would be completely contemporaneous with creation and identifiable with it. But it would not be the Creator that Christian faith describes. I do not for a moment pretend that the concept of God is an easy one to understand. Yet it is very important that, in trying to understand God, we describe the concept of God as well as we can.

In fact, the word 'God' can be misleading precisely because it is such a common word. It is a word that is used in all sorts of ways, for the most part without much reflection on its meaning. To begin to appreciate the problem of talking about the concept of 'God', we need to note first and foremost that we have almost no idea of what we are talking about.

It should be realised, further, that it is not possible for certain 'types' of God that we might have wished for to exist. For example, many say that they cannot accept a God who would tolerate pain and suffering in the world. The only God that can exist, however, is one whose existence is compatible with pain and suffering in the world, however difficult that may be for us to accept. This is so because pain and suffering are already found in the world. So, when a person says, 'I cannot believe in a God who would permit pain', that person is saying that he or she lays it down as a condition that there cannot be such a God. He or she takes it upon himself or herself to rule out the possibility of such a God existing. It seems to me that such a stance is less logical than one that is open to an acceptance of the God who does or who may exist and who can live, even in the short term, with human suffering.

There has never been a 'sighting' of this one God. No one has ever observed objectively an unseen power that embraces the whole universe and yet is utterly different and distinct from it. 'No one has ever seen God', as St John says.[2] The God whom we believe exists is very much a hidden God. Is there any evidence to suggest that such a being might exist? For the believer, the whole universe as it unfolds counts as evidence. The simplest plant in the ground that moves from seed to maturity and reproduction, to its eventual decline and death, counts as evidence. Yet many reject what exists as being evidence of God.

God: a being that is beyond everything

If God exists, then God has to be beyond anything that we are capable of reproducing in our minds. We live on a planet that we know, literally, to be a speck in a universe. It is a universe that consists of trillions of trillions of facts that are dissipated through all the spaces, the gases, the liquids and the solids of what is. It is, moreover, a universe that is, for now, constantly expanding. To have some knowledge of God, the believer must lift the mind beyond the existence of everything that can be encountered in the universe. Only then is it possible to consider what a creator might mean.

We know for certain that we exist. When I say 'we exist', I mean the human community as well as the animal world and what we see about us. When we reflect on the whole many-layered fabric of all existence, insofar as we can, or when, more likely, this whole perception intrudes on our consciousness unexpectedly, we may be in the presence of religious thought and feeling.

Religious thought arises from the 'why' question, as opposed to the 'how' question. Science is dominated by 'how' questions because these are the kind of questions it answers so well. It is at a complete loss when it comes to asking the ultimate 'why' ques-

---

2. John 1:17. In several places, the Old Testament refers to God as 'a hidden God'; see Is 45:15-26.

tions. Scientists themselves are the first to admit this. 'Why the universe?' is the biggest 'why' question that there is. The philosopher Liebniz asked: 'Why is it that there is something rather than nothing?'[3] When all the questions of science will have been answered, this question will remain.

'Why is it that there is something?' I see a young student cycling down the street without a care in the world, his scarf flying in the wind. He seems to have little care for 'why?' Why is he here? Why is he studying what he is studying? 'Why is it that there is anything?' This train of thought brings to mind the seemingly complete contingency of all things. And that seeming contingency of everything, that aspect of everything that looks so very dependent on chance, raises the question as to whether or not there is something that is not contingent, some one thing that is necessary, unconditional.

And why is it, furthermore, that a persistent question like 'why is it that there is something?' flashes before my mind when I least expect it to? We can say that the shafts of light that intervene suddenly in our thoughts, the questions that come from nowhere, are idle speculations that have no basis in a modern understanding of the world. Or we can allow the human imagination to have some space. Whether as believers or not, we can admit that we learn also from that which surprises us, which intrudes on our vision from beyond the confines of the experimental model of the universe. We can recognise in thoughts that spring on us and catch us unawares aspects of the world that we have overlooked or chosen to ignore. In other words, we can learn to recognise that these unexpected thoughts may be opportunities or invitations to reflect beyond the 'now'.

In our discussion of general knowledge, we saw how a kind of reflexive awareness took place in the mind that is very difficult to elucidate further. It is a kind of 'I know that I know'. Martin spoke of something very similar with regard to religious knowledge. He had already spoken to me of 'hanging on by the

---

3. For a popular treatment of Liebniz (1646-1716), see Bryan Magee, *The History of Philosophy*, London 1998, pp 96-99.

fingernails'. 'Perhaps the whole church is hanging on by the fingernails', I suggested:

> *Oh yes. The whole church is hanging on by the fingernails now. Absolutely. Oh, I have no doubt about that. Oh it is. It will change in time, and there's no doubt about it, it is hanging on at the moment in a big way. But at the end of it all I would have to say that the future is bright. You say: 'Why is that?' Because it is. I don't know why, but it is bright. Things will work out. At the end of all these things, you have to keep on saying: 'It will be alright, things will work out.' People will say: 'How do you know things will work out?' And you say: 'Just because they do work out'. You can't prove it, any more than you can prove the existence of God …*

It makes no sense to attempt to think of the infinite in terms of size. To say that God is 'bigger than …' is somehow to reduce him. Nor does it make any sense to think of the eternal in terms of age. God is ever young, as young as or, indeed, younger than the very last item of creation. At this level, the normally fluent faculty of reason breaks down. It is even a mistake to try to think of God as an idea. God is not only outside of the human mind but, as we have seen, he is beyond its unaided capacity.

Natural and supernatural

Well then, can it be shown that God actually exists and that he has communicated with us? As Christians we believe that God exists and that he has communicated with us, and that he does so today. Those who do not believe in God say that no God has spoken to us and that texts that purport to convey God to us are simply human inventions and nothing more than this. There is no way to resolve this divergence of view. In either case, at the observational level, there is what we might call a profound silence throughout the universe. We are free to take up one view or the other, and to attempt to accommodate our life to it.

As Christians, we are used to modes of thinking that, for reasons of clarity, insist on a sharp distinction being made between what can be known naturally and what can be known supernaturally. Natural knowledge refers to what is known only through the senses and through rational processes. Supernatural knowledge refers to what comes from God, which is the knowledge and confidence that accompanies faith. The traditional distinction between philosophy and theology, in Christian thought, is based on this separation, philosophy being the study of reality simply as it is, or as it appears to be, and theology being the study of the revealed word of God.

The same God, however, if there is a God, creates the natural world and the supernatural world. This same God of the natural and the supernatural has to be the God that we seek in the act of faith.

Natural observation and divine revelation go together in the act of religious belief. While these two spheres may be distinguished from each other, and they may be studied separately, yet, in the mind of the person who believes, they flow together and they belong together. They belong together in much the same way that observation and previous knowledge belong together in the act of perception. Observation of the natural world and supernatural knowledge received from God combine with each other in the act of faith.

The primary evidence that is available to us for the existence of God is the existence of this universe in which we live. It is in the context of the universe that God is understood broadly as God. This is the God who, we believe, has created us and who has communicated with us. Religious knowledge is as much about this earth and all that we experience as reality as it is about what God is.[4] While the word universe refers to all created things, it can also be accepted in an atheistic sense as referring simply to everything that is. But knowing God means knowing the world or the universe as God has revealed it to us, not simply as it may appear to be.

For this reason we need to integrate the question of God with

---

4. *'Since the creation of the world, the invisible things of God are understood through the things which have been made, and that his eternal power also and his divinity are valued through his works.'* St Ambrose c. 340-397, On the Mysteries, N 8, quoted in *The Divine Office,* Week 15 of the year, Monday.

the question of the world, even as we must distinguish between them. The principal reason for belief in God is belief in the world that God has made. It, the world, is already here. It is this world as it exists that gives rise to us who exist in it, and to our questions. The question of God (should God exist) and the questions of who we are, and what the world is, belong together.

According to Christian belief, then, there are two dimensions to creation, a natural dimension and a supernatural one. As Christians see it, both dimensions are required in order to reflect fully on what is. This reflection, or this correspondence between the mind and reality, is what Christians call truth.[5]

Yet this concept of truth causes difficulty for Declan.

You use the expression 'the truth' as though there is an answer to which one can progress through ultimately ... faith ... I don't know .... Again, I have a problem about this word truth, what do we mean by it? Truth is something that we can prove to ourselves ... 'That must be true ...' I can see a logical reason for it, I can see a historical reason for it, I can see a psychological reason for it ... and yes, one likes to reach for the truth, whatever that means ... again I wonder though, are we not falling back into this trap of our own constructs ... we have this thing which is demonstrable ... Q.E.D. 'the truth ...'.

From a Christian point of view, however, without forcing and without overlap, the natural and the supernatural dimensions of what God has made go together. To be in possession of the truth is to know the world as it is, broadly speaking. For Christians, knowledge of the truth includes the world as God has spoken it to us. In this sense, the natural and the supernatural occupy the same space.

---

5. *'What is truth?'* asked Pontius Pilate during the trial of Jesus (John 18:38). The definition that I have given here is sufficient for the purpose in hand. It has been in use since the time of Aristotle. For the purposes of my argument 'a genuine correspondence with all that is' can include valid knowledge that stems from our participation in culture, such as knowledge of human rights, as well as knowledge that stems from our observation of things.

A believing participant

I write from the place of faith; that is from a place where 'the two dimensions' of the universe are perceived; one dimension is perceived through the senses and the other perceived through the gift or the grace of faith. One dimension is natural and the other is supernatural. What I see, I see also with the 'eyes of faith'. What I judge, I judge also with the perspectives that faith brings. When I act, it is because faith has pre-disposed me to commit myself on the basis of evidence that I recognise has been laid before me by God.

Yet the very possibility of the gift of faith is often denied. It is held that the judgement of faith is always, of its very nature, an irrational one in the sense that it goes against reason. Faith, however, is not grounded in reason, even though reason is required to understand it. Faith transcends reason in somewhat the same way as the innocence of an accused person may be said to transcend the finding that a judge might make, or might not make, in favour of that person.[6]

Are people who deny the possibility of faith sufficiently open in this matter? Someone who denies the possibility of cruelty cannot be fair in a context where cruelty is the point at issue. You have to recognise what cruelty is before you can say whether or not a cruel act has taken place. In the same way, to be open on a question like faith in God, it seems that you have to be willing to recognise what faith in God might actually mean, even if you don't subscribe to it.

Some kind of openness does help in recognising what might count as evidence in seeking God. A fair observer would be the first to admit that only something like faith makes it possible to be in touch with a God who is invisible and beyond any direct observation. Such an observer would have to admit that there could be a possibility, however remote it might seem, that people who say that they are in touch with God have this sense of

---

6. *University Sermons*, op. cit., X , 'Faith and Reason, contrasted as habits of mind', pp 182-3.

contact in some way that is grounded both in God's gift and in their own judgement of this gift.[7]

The admission that something like faith in God could lead to a discovery of God is very important. It indicates an attitude of openness to God, even if that openness is not yet faith. Many people find themselves unable to come even thus far. Both Declan and Suzanne consider that it is impossible to get beyond our own rational experience of the world and make judgements about what they are convinced is not there.

The act of faith is basically an acceptance on the believer's part of the testimony of God. The knowledge of God that follows upon the act of faith includes much assumed information that, in the ordinary course of events, we take from each other. The fact that it is assumed knowledge is neither here nor there. It is in this sense like most knowledge; possession of it inevitably implies a certain dependence on others that have preceded us. All ordinary and specialised religious knowledge is both assumed and acquired knowledge.

As we have seen earlier, the very structure of knowledge is such that a form of belief precedes all knowledge. To say the least, we trust in our senses and in our own judgement. It is possible to say that knowing any person is, in a manner of speaking, like knowing God. But while the manner of our knowing of religion and of other matters that are wholly secular is very similar, it is not so with the object (God) of religious knowledge. The object of religious knowledge, that is, what is known about God, is utterly unique. It is unique in that this knowledge comes to us ultimately, we believe, by way of a revelation from God. Hence we refer to the object of religious knowledge as a gift.

What we hear from others is as important, if not more so, than what we see with our own eyes.[8] My knowledge of God and of the world includes matters of doctrine, the statements

---

7. See *Grammar of Assent*, op. cit., pp 97-109.

8. The contrast between 'seeing' and 'hearing' is a favourite theme in scripture. See, for example, Xavier Leon-Dufour, *Dictionary of Biblical Theology*, London 1967, articles 'Listen' and 'See'. In his *Sermons on Subjects of the Day*, op. cit., VI 'Faith and Experience', pp 74-75, Newman

that we find in the creeds, the precepts of the 'ten commandments' and many other details. All of this is to be expected.
Perhaps, it is because religious knowledge is 'revealed' knowledge that it fits in so exactly with the ordinary processes by
which we come to know. Naming God is not unlike coming to
know that we are free human beings. It is at once obvious, and
yet it is elusive. It is like knowing the dignity of every human
being; you cannot prove it, yet you can know it.

To name God is, I believe, to begin to know God. This knowing of God is quite irreducible, and it comes from the gift of
grace in the individual soul. It belongs to that knowing that accompanies trust and confidence and love. When someone sincerely ventures upon the act of faith in trust and in confidence,
they find that they are themselves 'apprehended' by the other
whom we call 'God'.[9] What began for them as darkness and uncertainty, begins to become for them certainty and conviction,
even when, to a greater or a lesser extent, the darkness persists.

For Christians, religious faith admits a person to knowledge
that has been revealed to the human race by God, its creator. We
cannot see God, yet we have some human images that tell us
something of his likeness. These images come from God. And
we have, further, a man who claimed to be a disclosure of God,
one who claimed to have been raised from the dead. That is the

_____

makes a great play on this distinction: '... *to insist on a point which is very
important, the necessity we lie under, if we would be Christians indeed, of
drawing our religious notions and views, not from what we see, but from what
we do not see, but only hear; or rather, the great mistake under which men of
the world lie, of judging of religious subjects merely by what the experience of
life tells them ... On the other hand, the very ground from which religious men
start, is the avowal that the sights of this world are against them, and that they
must believe in God in spite of this.*'
9. We get a sense of this being apprehended by God in the following
prayer of St. Anselm: '*Teach me to seek you, and reveal yourself to me as I
seek, because I can neither seek you if you do not teach me how, nor find you
unless you reveal yourself. Let me seek you in desiring you; let me desire you in
seeking you; let me find you in loving you; let me love you in finding you.*'
Proslogion of St Anselm, ch. 1, quoted in *The Divine Office*, Advent, week
1, Friday.

message of Christianity. In the next two chapters, we will look at these links with God more closely. For now, we need simply to hold to the connection that exists between religious knowledge and the self-disclosure of God.

CHAPTER SIX

Revelation and Knowledge of God

Revelation, Christians believe, does not originate with the human race. It is a self-disclosure by God to humanity. Therefore, we may reasonably expect to be somewhat surprised by it and by what it contains. If we take the identity of Jesus Christ as the saviour of his people as a particular instance of revelation, this element of surprise and unexpectedness becomes very evident. Throughout the long history of the Jewish people it was widely accepted that a promised leader was awaited. He would be sent by God to restore Israel to its glory. Yet, when Jesus came, he was not the messiah that many had anticipated. Even some of his own disciples and apostles found him difficult to accept at this level. He was cruelly and savagely put to death in advance of the feast of the Passover at Jerusalem in or about the year 33 AD.

Yet, when the first Christians looked back through all that had been written of the messiah in their own Jewish tradition, what they found was the figure of Christ. In prophecies, psalms and texts, for hundreds of years, he was there in all but name. Not only did they find Christ, the Saviour, foreshadowed, but they found also his passion and death. Certainly, it was only in the context of the Jesus that they now knew that many of these references became plausible. Something happened in the time following the death of Jesus that convinced his followers beyond all doubt that he was the son of God and that he was the messiah that was to come, expected or not. Mark, Luke and John all tell of an extended period when the risen Jesus instructed his disciples after his death. This experience, for most of them, seems to have been the turning point of revelation.

It is not that the prophetic references in the Old Testament make a complete case for what we believe Jesus to be. Rather they confirm a judgement that is made on more basic grounds. It seems to the believer that Jesus is, in every sense, the most perfect image or impression or understanding of what God himself is like, humanly speaking. The more familiar we become with the traditions and texts of the Old Testament and with everything that has been recorded and passed on to us about Jesus, the more that we can recognise the intertwining of the identities of God and of Jesus.

Many times in the Old Testament, God had indeed promised that he would come to the aid of his people, that he would be their shepherd, that he would be the gardener that would tend his own vine. But the idea that God would himself assume a human form and become an actual person in the world was not one that was contemplated. In ancient times, this was a surprising and shocking conclusion. It is no less so in our world today.

It is said that Jesus came to save us from our sins. This is the other surprise that was completely unexpected although not unannounced in the scriptures. The whole anticipation of Jesus' contemporaries was focused on some figure who would rally the people against the Romans at that time and lead them to resounding victory. In fact, this messiah came to deliver the people, all peoples, Romans included, from their false selves. That is still what Christianity offers today. Yet today, as ever, many are unable or unwilling to contemplate a salvation of this kind.

In this chapter, I want to look at the hard facts, such as they are, that support Christian belief. This entails an examination of the concept of a living revelation from several different angles. It seems to many people that the very possibility of a divine revelation is impossible. To others, who may be more open to such a possibility, questions arise as to how it could take place and how could it be validated. It is interesting to note that we are told in the gospel text of St Luke that Mary, the mother of Jesus, on the occasion of the annunciation, raised key issues concerning revelation.

There arise many other particular aspects about the content of revelation that are surprising and remarkable. If any of what fol-

lows is at first difficult to understand, I would ask that the reader
stay with it and turn it over in his or her mind. All of the people
who were first involved with God's communication of himself to
us have had to do just this.

On the concept of revelation
The culture in which we live has set its face against the very possibility of revelation. The scientific worldview that dominates much
of modernity and post-modernity excludes any real notion of the
miraculous in the sense in which that word is used in the gospels;
it excludes any possibility that something like a divine intervention can ever take place. According to this view, there is nothing
divine to intervene, and hence the world is a more or less pre-
dictable place.

Paradoxically, again according to this view, it is only in science
that anything that is like a miracle can be considered. From the
point of view of science, the whole of underlying reality is now
thought to be unpredictable, as we have noted in chapter four.
According to 'small particle' physics, a study that has developed
with the discovery of the atom, the so-called 'uncertainty principle' brings this out clearly. So, in one sense, it appears that nothing at all can be predicted about reality at this level. The 'miraculous' may still be very much with us, but it is now in the service of
science, not religion. That is, once 'miracle' is framed in scientific
terms, it becomes perfectly acceptable to modernity.

Within this context, I am aware of the strangeness to the modern ear of talk about revelation. We have reached a stage where
many people are no longer sure that they actually believe that
God exists, never mind whether or not he has spoken. We seldom
reflect on the degree to which God has been written out of modern speech. It is not unlike the situation that feminists speak of
with regard to women in history. It could be said that God is excluded from 'official speech' today in much the same way that the
female voice is perceived to have been excluded from official
speech in days gone by. Yet God is with us now, I believe, as
women were with us then.

One of the unfortunate effects of this change has been the

growth of an element of defensiveness in religious belief. People tend to think that revelation must mean that some blinding disclosure from the heavens has happened. Understandably, this impression of revelation is frequently ridiculed as a crass image. Often, it is felt that to be a believer one has to subscribe to such an image, or to attempt to defend it. This, as we will see, is far from the case. In fact, what we believe about revelation is a very subtle and moderate doctrine. The picture that is portrayed by revelation arises, almost seamlessly, from the ancient world in which this communication took place. This seamless presence of revelation remains in our world today.

Our culture is heavily impregnated with the evidence of God's communication with us, although it might not seem so at first glance. Many of our everyday accepted points of reference are rooted in the assumption that there is a God and that he has spoken to us. Even the year on the ordinary calendar in the Christian world has been traditionally fixed by reckoning on when Christ lived. At the level of each week, moreover, we find that Sunday is 'the Lord's day' and, hence, 'the day of rest'; this is only because it is the day on which it is believed that Jesus was raised from the dead. The whole idea of a 'day of rest' each week comes from our Jewish heritage where the 'Sabbath' represented the seventh day on which God rested from his work of creation. Perhaps there is no more public witness than these facts to the event of revelation. In other words, it has been widely believed in the world that God has spoken to us, and that God's only son Jesus lived and died, and that he was raised from the dead.

It may be that dates and days may undergo some further alteration as they have in the more distant past. Perhaps, for all we know, the 'Christian witness' of the calendar will go. What cannot change is the fact that, for four thousand years, AD and BC, a significant portion of humanity has believed and understood that God has communicated with it. That portion of humanity consists firstly of the Jews, then the Christians and, later, the Muslims. And despite the social, technological and political changes that have taken place in that length of time, particularly the changes that we have witnessed in our own generation, the description of life and of humanity that we find in revelation is one that resonates largely with our own experience. There is infinitely more however: in revelation we are actually told something about God. Nowhere else, for believers, is such real information to be found.

Revelation, because it is communicated among believers in such multifaceted ways, is not always well served by religion. We have rituals and ceremonies that are frequently rushed or misunderstood and sermons we ought never have to hear. There are clergy who are less than good and supposedly sincere believers who fall far short of the ideals spoken of by Jesus. The public face of God's revealed word is, after some four thousand years, not always attractive. Open talk about any love, for example, can appear as banality. When it is talk of the love of God, it can invite ridicule. It might often seem that the believer, an actual person going into a church and kneeling down to pray, belongs more to the theatre of the absurd rather than to the actual world in which we live.

We need to understand sympathetically the concept and the content of what has been revealed by God. It may be better to stand back from the many voices that would speak to us of revelation. No one has ever seen God, St John reminds us.[1] The Hebrew faith was predicated on the witness of certain chosen figures, notably Abraham, Moses and the prophets of Israel. Each of these was given to understand, in a manner that was possible for someone of that particular generation, that God existed and that he cared for those whom he had called to worship him. We can see that this understanding was often contradicted directly by the society in which it was received. The texts of the Old Testament, as of the New, are cast in a way that leaves the reader in no doubt as to the difficulty of communicating the divine message to people who do not want to listen.

The Christian faith, which flows directly from the Hebrew faith, is predicated on the witness of Jesus Christ. Jesus is a unique

---

1. See 1 John 4:12 & par.

human witness to revelation. He is revelation in the sense that, even 'from the beginning',[2] it is he who is and was and will be the word of God. Christians believe that it is he, Jesus, who stands behind the faith of Abraham and Moses and the prophets of the Old Testament. Ultimately, we believe, it is from him that all faith stems.

We believe that Jesus is utterly trustworthy as God's witness, and that he communicates that trustworthiness of his to those who really follow him. And it is always from such a person, from the sincere follower as well as from Jesus himself, that we, in our turn, receive the gift of faith. This is one sense of the phrase '… where two or three are gathered in my name, there am I in the midst of them.'[3] The gift of faith turns upon the fact of a revealing God who has spoken and whose spoken word is embodied in his divine Son and in the community of believers.

The 'written word' of God

The texts of the Bible are not things from outside that have been 'dropped' upon humanity. Sacred scripture is something that has grown and developed organically from within human history and within the lives of ordinary men and women.[4] As we might have expected, the common knowledge of the ancient world as it was known at that time is the knowledge that we find in the scriptures. This organic development took place within culture and within the context of the hopes and fears of those people among whom the 'seed' of the word was sown.

The texts are a series of writings, some seventy books as we now have them but originally probably many more, that have been sewn together and blended into each other. They are, moreover, extremely varied in character and they bear within them all

2. These words introduce the Bible, Genesis 1:1, and also the gospel of John.
3. Mt 18:20.
4. A brief summary of the Catholic understanding of the nature of the scriptures is to be found in *Dogmatic Constitution on Divine Revelation*, Ch 3: 11, 12, 13, in *The Documents of Vatican II*, London-Dublin 1966, pp 118-121.

the marks and traits of the ancient culture from which they have come down to us. On almost every important matter that they consider, whether it be the creation of the world, or the exodus of the chosen people from Egypt sometime in the second millennium BC, or the handing down of the Ten Commandments, or the making and remaking of a sacred covenant between God and his people, or the important historical developments that took place subsequently in Israel, there are several versions all from different hands.

In the New Testament, moreover, there are four gospels, not one; and the accounts overlap, and in some minor respects do not even agree with each other. The word 'gospel' means, originally, 'good news'. In addition to the gospels, there are the Acts of the Apostles and the epistles ascribed to Peter, John, Paul and others. Many of these predate the actual gospels. In other words, for something like two or three generations or perhaps more, the Christian faith was lived and practised without any normative text in a written sense. In fact, some three centuries passed before it was decided finally which writings were to be included in the 'canon' of scripture, that is, in the actual list of writings that were held to be inspired by God and which were to count as 'revelation'.

The Bible contains very much more than accounts of things. There is poetry, prayer, prophecy, parable, story, law, exhortation, interrogation of history, questioning of God, to name but some of the literary genres and forms that are found there. Many of these types are found in both the Old and the New Testaments. The Old Testament covers something like two millennia, not to mention the creation narrative which purports to address what we might call 'pre-history'. The New Testament, on the other hand, centres largely on one human life – that of Jesus. For this reason, it is more focused in every respect.

We find also in the Bible many 'verbal' images of God that are taken up in a culture where it was forbidden to have any 'stone' or 'wooden' image of God. For example, God is variously portrayed imaginatively as father, judge and warrior, among others. Many of these images are later cast aside as inadequate as more perceptive impressions of who and what 'God' might be gained hold on the minds of the people.

The Hebrew idea of God is very different from notions of God that were current elsewhere in the ancient world. This God is a 'hidden God', a God who of his very nature is invisible and, without his help, impossible of discovery. The early Christians were frequently persecuted for being 'atheists' in the Roman Empire. Rather than being atheists, their belief was in the hidden God of the Jews who had revealed himself in the man Jesus.

What emerges from a study of the scriptures is an awareness of how the texts each correct and interpret one another. In a very real sense, the message of revelation is a message that flows from a shared and informed reading of what we find there. And that is how it has been understood from the very beginning. That is why there can be no univocal interpretation that is drawn from only one text of scripture. There is no place for 'fundamentalism' in revelation, that is, where one word or text is understood apart from its whole context and held up as a sacred norm. Nor is there any merit in that 'liberalism' that is always willing to dispense with the meanings of religious texts and seeks explanations only in purely rational sources.

Various attempts have been made to describe what the message of God might be in its fullness. These are negative definitions putting down necessary limits along the edges of revelation. The Christians of the third century decided that God's revelation came to an end with the death of the last apostle. Nobody knows when that death took place or which apostle it was. What we do know is that, at that time, the community, or the 'church', was confident that there was now a boundary within which revelation could be understood. The picture that had been communicated up to that point was already an infinite treasure. It was held to be endlessly capable of generating understanding of God and of his creation throughout the course of human history.

The Catholic Church claims that it holds revelation in its fullness. This claim states only that the picture that was handed on in the apostolic generation is the same living picture as is available in the believing community today. In other words, it is a claim that 'it is all there.' It is a claim that is made by a branch of the Christian family that traces its roots directly to the apostles. Furthermore, the fact that revelation has been already transmitted to us is something that can easily slip past our modern awareness. We need to recognise that God has already spoken long before any of us become capable of hearing the message that awaits us. It is 'all there'; it has all happened. The word 'revelation' points to the fact that something has been revealed, and it refers us to the content of what has been revealed.

This sense of revelation as something that has already taken place can go some way to explaining the 'conservatism' that one finds in Catholicism. Church leaders tend to be very conscious of that which they have 'received'. Reminding his readers of the institution of the Blessed Eucharist by Jesus, St Paul writes: 'For I received from the Lord what I also delivered to you, that the Lord Jesus on the night when he was betrayed took bread …'[5] The Latin root 'tradito' translates into the English 'I delivered'. It is the same word Paul uses when referring to his handing on to others of his belief in the resurrection.[6] The link with 'tradition' becomes immediately obvious.

Yet, as we will see, development of the tradition is also of huge importance. Tradition is not a dead thing. It has life and is capable of 'legitimate' and 'consistent' growth in much the same way as a human body.[7] That is why Christians subscribe to what they believe is an ongoing developing tradition, guaranteed by the

---

5. 1 Cor 15:1-6ff.
6. 1 Cor 11:23-26.
7. The analogy is from the first notebook of Vincent of Lerins, chap 23. He was a priest and monk of the fifth century who died before 450. Quoted in *The Divine Office* III, week 27, Friday. The clear articulation of the development of doctrine is one of the insights that John Henry Newman brought to the church on the occasion of his conversion to it in 1845. See his *Essay on the Development of Christian Doctrine*, London, 1845.

divine guidance of the Holy Spirit, capable of sustaining an understanding of the scriptures in every age.

It is possible to overlook, unintentionally, the fact that the gift of Christian faith has been held, nurtured and developed in the church for some two thousand years. Which of us, on receiving something very precious from God, would not want to handle that gift with the greatest respect? This would be especially so in contexts where the content and the right understanding of that gift tend to be subjects of dispute and contention. In this sense, revelation is something that binds us, as well as something that liberates us.

Revelation is a message that shines out when we consider 'in faith' the scriptural data that is laid before us. It is a light that becomes 'word made flesh' in the person of Jesus Christ and in the life that he lived and the death that he endured. That light, for the believer, flashes most insistently in the doctrine of the resurrection of Jesus from the dead.

The Holy Spirit

The on-going understanding of Revelation led in early times to the formulation that there were three persons in one God, Father, Son, and Holy Spirit. The Holy Spirit is the third 'person' of God, Jesus being described as the second and the Father as the first. This 'person' is linked to the whole concept of 'divine inspiration', the guiding hand of God in human affairs. It is this divine person that is associated particularly with the work of advocating and living the gospel. Belief in the Spirit connects each Christian to the importance of God's people on earth.

In the Old Testament and in the New, it is clear that the people are the carriers of the message, even before the texts themselves are. It is the 'church' or the ancient Christian community that has written down, and selected, and preserved the 'inspired' texts. This identification between the 'Spirit' and 'community' is central to revelation. The Spirit has come down upon God's people, on Jesus at his baptism in the river Jordan, on Mary and on the apostles at the first Pentecost, and upon every Christian in the sacraments of baptism and of confirmation. God does not speak into a void; the word of God has always been a 'living' word, living and springing up in the hearts of men and women who 'hear it and keep it'.[8]

One way of beginning to appreciate this depth in God's creation and the pervasiveness of the Holy Spirit of God is to reflect on the symbolic language that is found in the scriptures and in the liturgy of the church. The symbolism of the language with which God communicates with us is a vital aspect of the contact that is made and sustained. When the word 'water' is used in the scripture, whether as a source of life or as a symbol of eternal freshness and purity, we should be aware of the role that water plays in the parched desert lands of the Bible.[9] When we speak of being immersed in water, as at baptism, or when Jesus refers to himself as the 'living water' that springs up in the human soul, what is meant is something alive, fresh and almost tangible. It is the same with 'bread' and 'wine'. These words immediately convey a sense of human conversation that is alive, that is happening. Within the symbolism of bread and wine, we believers find the reality of the body and the blood of Christ that is offered for us.

And so it is throughout the scriptures. When we read that God is a shepherd, we must understand just that. God, Jesus, cares for us, even with his own life. We are, each of us, that important to him. We are perfectly entitled to make the earthy comparison that this image invites with any shepherd who rears and cares for his sheep during the heat and drought or during the harsh winter and the frosty spring. When we read that we are with Jesus one vine, we are invited to look at the stock, the branches, the leaf and the fruit. We are invited to see and to feel the image, and to sense the disappointment where there is no fruit. That is the meaning of symbolic language.

The revealed word of God speaks to us also about ourselves. All of the personalities of the scriptures, the good and the bad, are

---

8. See, for example, Mt 12:46-50; Is 55:10-11.
9. Leon Dufour, op. cit. See the entries for Water, Bread, Wine, Shepherd and Flock, Vine.

instructive for us. They reflect our own personalities back to us. We can check into stories, psalms, parables and preaching and we can find that we ourselves are already there. Part of the veracity of the apostle Peter, the fisherman who had a mother-in-law, a house and, presumably, a family, is surely what I can recognise of myself in him.[10] Part of the veracity of the story of the sisters Martha and Mary and their brother Lazarus, who welcomed Jesus into their home and questioned him, is what I recognise of my own life in their lives.[11] Part of the veracity of Pontius Pilate, the governor who finally washed his hands, literally, of the innocent Jesus, is what I recognise about my own conscience in his conscience.[12] The fact that our culture has been formed on the Bible may account for some of this ease of identification. Believers, however, identify with the people in the Bible because they accept it is the revealed word of God. If the sacred text is a revelation to us of the nature of God, it is equally and, at the same time, a revelation to us about ourselves.

The person of Jesus

The person of Jesus addresses us from the pages of the gospels. Do we trust and believe him? This, ultimately, is the question upon which faith depends. It was Jesus who spoke to us about God as father.[13] The Aramaic word 'Abba', in our terms 'Papa', was the name he used. It was Jesus who claimed that he spoke in the name of God when others accused him of blasphemy: 'I say to you your sins are forgiven'.[14] It was Jesus who performed miracles and works the like of which had not been seen before: 'the blind see, the lame walk and the poor have the good news preached to them'.[15] It was Jesus who said to the good thief: 'today you will be with me in paradise'.[16] It was Jesus who cried

10. Mt 8:14-15.
11. See Jn 11.
12. Mt 27:24.
13. See Mt 6:9-13 & par.
14. Mt 9:2-6 & par.
15. Mt 11:5 & par.
16. Lk 23:43.

out on the cross: 'My God, My God, why have you forsaken me?'[17] It is very likely that at that moment he was praying the words of psalm 21, the prayer of a man 'on a cross' spoken in agony. Then, we are told that Jesus rose from the dead on the third day, as he had said he would do.[18] Do we believe those who told us that it is so, even if we cannot fully understand everything that this may mean? Do we believe in 'him'? Are we willing to trust 'him'?

The person of Jesus is to be distinguished from many representations of him. The world abounds with his image, sacred and profane, solemn and casual. Since Roman times, his name has been scribbled, drawn, painted, carved, cursed, sworn in every place on earth, in every chapel, in every tavern. Who was this man? Is it possible that we can find out for ourselves who he was? Yes, it is possible.

The person that emerges from the pages of the New Testament is credible. Some of these texts were written by his own disciples and apostles, people who had themselves witnessed the events that they describe. Many of these 'texts' or sayings already existed in some formalised oral form before they came to be written down. That is how 'news' was transmitted in first century Palestine. Language studies shows us today that oral transmission is an utterly reliable form of transmission in some early communities and cultures. It can confidently be asserted that the decision that faced the early readers of these texts is no different from the decisions that confront us today. We find that we ourselves are asking the same questions as they did. The basic question is, for us as for them, 'who is he?'

Not everybody who saw and heard Jesus believed him to be genuine. The New Testament is very clear about this. Apart from those who condemned him, there were a great many people who remained unconvinced by his claims. We are told that the crowd called out for him to be crucified.[19] On another occasion, we are

---

17. Mt 27:46; Ps 22:1.
18. Mk 8:31; 9:31; 10:34 & par.
19. Mt 27:23.

told that the people of his own village, perhaps even members of his extended family, did not believe in him.[20] Several others believed in him secretly, like Nicodemus who came to him under cover of darkness.[21] One man is reported as saying: 'I believe, help my unbelief.'[22]

We should remember the 'hidden God' of Israel's belief. Given the events as they are reported to have happened, the picture that builds up before us is not unreal. It was the apostle Peter who said: 'I do not know the man.'[23] This same Peter is reported as saying on another occasion: 'You are the Christ the Son of the living God.'[24] Which Peter do we believe? Can we believe both of them? Can we believe the Peter who broke down and who wept?[25] These different and contradictory states of the same Peter have about them a remarkable ring of authenticity.

Two of the writings of the New Testament are ascribed to the hand of this Peter.[26] He is the one whom Jesus named as head of the apostles and to whom he gave the second name, 'Rock'.[27] In the scriptures this was a name that had been given only to God.[28] Peter, 'Rock', is a key figure, both before and after the death of Jesus. With Mary Magdalene,[29] he is a prime witness to the resurrection of Jesus. It was she who announced the resurrection to the others, and it was he who led the way in preaching boldly throughout Jerusalem and Judea the message that Jesus had risen from the dead. This resurrection of Jesus, together with his death on the cross, convinces many that, in him, something strange and wonderful and eternal was at work. For others, these events are the great 'stumbling block' that impedes their would-be faith.

20. Mt 11:57.
21. Jn 3:2.
22. Mk 9:24.
23. Mt 26:72 & par.
24. Mt 16:16.
25. Mt 26:75 & par.
26. 1 & 2 Peter.
27. Mt 16:18.
28. Deut 32:4; Pss 18:2, 31; 28:1; 31:2, 3; 42:9; 89:26; 92:15; 95:2; 144:1.
29. Mt 28:1-10.

It was to Peter and to the apostle James that the earliest Christian communities looked for leadership. This Peter was well aware of the difficulties of Christian belief. In his second letter we read Peter's response to those who questioned when Jesus was to return in glory:

'Well, when is this coming (the return of Jesus)? *Everything goes on as it has since the Fathers died, as it has since it began at the creation …'* and Peter answers: *'But there is one thing, my friends, that you must never forget: that with the Lord, a 'day' can mean a thousand years, and a thousand years is like a day.'* [30]

After Paul had been converted to the faith that he had been persecuting, he went up to Jerusalem to speak with Peter and clarify matters of contention that had arisen in his own teaching. Paul tells us that on one issue he 'withstood him (Peter) to the face',[31] because of what Paul felt was Peter's timidity before some of his own people. As tradition tells it, and it is very reliable, this Peter died on a cross in or about the city of Rome sometime about the year 55 AD and he is buried there.[32]

This following of the trail of Peter is one of hundreds, perhaps thousands, of entry points into the story that the New Testament puts before us. Jesus asks Peter at Caesarea Philippi: 'But who do you say that I am?'[33]

The story of the New Testament is always the story of Jesus and that story always culminates in the same question being posed to the reader: 'But who do you say that I am?' There is no other body of writing that comes down to us in human history that addresses us in this way. It is the narrative of Jesus that speaks to us. It is his birth, his life, his death and his resurrection from the dead; it is his claim for himself and for God, his 'Abba'.

---

30. 2 Pet 3:4, 8.
31. Gal 2:11.
32. See for example, *New Catholic Encyclopedia*, Second Edition, Washington DC, 2003, Vol II, 'Peter, Apostle, Saint', (J. J. Castelot) 173-176; and Vol 14, 'Vatican', (F. X. Murphy, C. Kosanke) The Tomb and Bones of Peter, 390-391.
33. Mt. 16. 15.

This is his message for humankind. This, in its totality and in its detail, is what is meant by the revelation of God.[34]

To be seized by the revelation, to find that one is questioned by it, or perplexed by it, or that there is cause to revise any of our assumptions on the basis of it, or to be consoled by some aspect of it: this is what the phrase 'God has spoken to me' means.

Our personal judgement

What is our own judgement about the significance of Jesus? The question must be faced by anyone who has heard of the gospel. Do we see only the wandering preacher, the wonder-worker, 'He saved others ... he cannot save himself';[35] or do we see beyond the appearances to the gift from God that is enclosed in this life and in this death, and that usually only gradually reveals itself to those who are ready and willing to receive it?

Suzanne saw religious belief as very convenient for the believer but not at all realistic for the modern person. We have seen already her description of faith as a projection. The reader might unconsciously transfer this impression to the realities of history.

It is a very handy projection, and it is a very nice projection, but I find it particularly difficult to believe. In terms of after-life, I'd probably be more sympathetic towards the idea of re-incarnation than I would to the green pastures in heaven which are in the clouds. I know that's extreme ... and I know not everybody thinks that simplistically. But everyone has his own different sort of version of what it might be.

Christians readily accept that all primitive religions have elements of projection in them, and that indeed the faith of many believers in Jesus Christ is not without elements of projection also. But the Christian faith is based on something that really happened in history, in a series of events that have been written down and passed on to us. Hence, in this case, belief in God is inextricably linked with what we know has really happened.

The events of Christian history can be studied, studied as wit-

---

34. See Hans Urs Von Balthasar, *The Glory of the Lord*, Edinburgh, 1982, Vol 1, pp 131ff for an extended treatment of our knowledge of God.
35. Mt 27:42 & par.

nesses saw them, some of whom believed and others of whom did not believe. So it is a history that in some measure stands up to objective scrutiny. At the trial of Jesus, Peter saw and Pilate saw; yet Peter's recollection was one of faith, while we assume that Pilate's was not.

In the case of the resurrection of Jesus from the dead, St Matthew speaks of one occasion when many disciples saw Jesus at one time. Yet, among these, he is careful to point out, there were some who doubted.[36] What are we to make of this? It does not seem as if there can be a neutral category or group who neither believe nor suspend belief indefinitely, given the evidence. Once Thomas was shown the wounds of Christ, for example, he then believed.[37] Matthew's motive was one of preaching the 'good news' as accurately as he could. There were clearly some who did not believe; he says this. Yet the evidence that most people believed, on that occasion, is evidence that those of us who are influenced by Matthew can accept. We can accept it because we accept Matthew; we share his belief.

The life of Jesus, and hence many of the questions that it raises, occurred in history. This is what historians agree to; and this agreement places the life of Jesus at a time and a place. So Christianity cannot be understood simply as the projection of some human myth. People who believed saw the risen Jesus while there were others with them who did not see and who were not convinced. In the very nature of the case, it seems that faith judgements are required, both then and now, in respect of what is transmitted. There is no way of avoiding this issue that confronts us as much today as it confronted those in ancient times. It is an issue that turns upon the 'miraculous' in history.

In my conversation with Martin, I was struck by his seeming indifference to the study of theology. I asked him about the creeds of the church, whether they played any role in his faith:

'No, very little, very little.'

I then asked him about the Catechism:

36. Mt 28:17.
37. Jn 20:24.

'Eh … I remembered bits of the Catechism for years and years, of course, but insofar as they had any effect, no, its almost gone.'

I asked about the Blessed Trinity:

'Very little … the only things that mean anything to me are phrases from the Old and New Testaments, stories of faith and of trust and of loyalty.'

With the next question, however, I came upon a response that was very different to these. I asked about the resurrection to which he replied:

'Hugely important. Everything … like St Paul, without the resurrection, without the risen Christ, there is no … there is nothing, there is no Christianity. And yet that phenomenon itself is not so remarkable when you think … it's like people say: 'the incarnation, sure that is all old rubbish …' as if the Lord, the God who created the world, couldn't implant a baby seed in a young woman in Israel two thousand years ago without any third party involvement. You might as well say: 'well, that flower, where did it come from, where did that tree come from, where did those seeds come from? …'

'So the resurrection and the incarnation are at a similar level for you?'

'That's right. I mean they have to be. I think if we could become more aware of the nearness of the Lord and his doings in Jerusalem, in Nazareth and in the Holy Land generally, I think we would become much more aware of the nearness of God.'

These remarks illustrate to me the basic truths that I have been trying to set out in this chapter. They are that revelation comes from God not from man; that revelation is bound to surprise us rather than to confirm us in our own knowledge of the world; that revelation, for all its diversity and antiquity, is centred on the person of Jesus, on his life, his death and his resurrection.

CHAPTER SEVEN

Who is this Jesus?

According to the Christian faith, there are two claims that Jesus is believed to have made for himself. The first is that he was the Son of God in the sense of being an incarnation of God on earth. The second claim is that, in and through his life, death and resurrection, what is called 'the paschal mystery' of Jesus, the power of evil in the world and in history is somehow overcome. By this means the 'salvation' of humanity is said to take place. In other words, Jesus claims to be someone who is at the level of God in his own person and being. He offers us a 'supernatural' view of life that is inclusive of everything in our experience, including good and evil. He promises a resolution to come, in paradise, of our experience in this life on earth.

The opening of the Letter to the Hebrews, an ancient community of Christian Jews, reads as follows:

In many and various ways God spoke of old to our fathers by the prophets; but in these last days he has spoken to us by a Son, whom he appointed the heir of all things, through whom also he created the world. He reflects the glory of God and bears the very stamp of his nature, upholding the universe by his word of power. When he had made purification for sins, he sat down at the right hand of the Majesty on high, having become as much superior to angels as the name he has obtained is more excellent than theirs.[1]

This is just one example of many similar quotations that could be given from the New Testament. It is a quotation that testifies to the earliest beliefs of Christians. It shows clearly the two claims that have been mentioned, the first in relation to

---

1. Heb 1:1-4.

Jesus being 'a Son' of God in a very unique sense, and the second in relation to the work of 'purification for sins' that Jesus undertook. Other choices of text would illustrate these two themes equally well.[2]

In looking at these claims, we should remind ourselves that what was known about God in the time of Jesus was already revealed knowledge. The Jewish people were heirs to the word of God. It was they, and at that time they alone, who had such a highly developed sense of the uniqueness of God. It was they who believed in a God that could not be imaged by us in any way. It was they who, believing in such a God, believed that this God had revealed something of himself to them. It was they who looked forward to the coming of a 'messiah', that is someone whom this God would send to deliver the people from their enemies.

As we have already seen, no one had imagined that the messiah who was to come would be, in fact, God himself. With the benefit of hindsight, we can now look back, as the authors of the New Testament did, and see an outline of the coming Christ in various parts of the sacred writings. Moreover, this theme of the condemned Christ is very evident.[3] Like those authors did, we can recognise, in particular, the picture of the condemned Christ already sketched out and embedded in writings that scholars reckon are from a figure whom they call 'deutero-Isaiah'. This author lived some six to five centuries before the Christian era and his work was then inserted into the eighth century BC Isaiah,[4] a very much older book. In other words, the text was fitted into an earlier one.

The knowledge that had already been revealed is very significant. It is the revelation of what we would term a 'monotheistic' God; namely, that there is only one God, not a plurality of Gods.

---

2. For example: Rom 1:3-4; Col 1:15-20; Phil 2:5-11; Jn 1:14; 1 Jn 1:1ff. See Aloys Grillmeier SJ, *Christ in Christian Tradition*, London 1965, chap 1, pp 3-35.
3. One of the most familiar of these is Ps 22.
4. See Is 42:1-7; 49:1-9; 50:4-9; 52:13-53. 12, and note on Isaiah in the *Jerusalem Bible*, p 1124.

Not only this is revealed. It is clearly stated that, from the beginning of creation, this God is a wholly distinct creator. God is not
in any sense a part or an aspect of the universe. God is a personal
being who comes to us from outside of all 'existence' as we can
know it.

An incomprehensible claim?

Some might say that the claim of Jesus to divinity was quite in-
comprehensible to the Hebrew mind. This was one reason why
he was put to death. The gospels remind us on several occasions
how circumspect Jesus was in articulating this claim to divinity.
We can see this in the trial of Jesus before the High Priest and before Pilate as recounted by John.[5] It was a claim that might have
found an easier acceptance in the context of some pagan religions where Gods were many. The claim must be understood,
however, in the context of the Jewish religion which we believe
to be a revealed religion. This claim held that what God had already revealed was now being further developed, opened up, to
provide more information about the very nature of God. This
further information was, and is, we believe, part of God's plan
for every human being.

We need to stand back and look at the revelation of God as a
whole piece, Old Testament and New Testament. We need to
ask whether the information that is provided there about the
world and about God, including information about Jesus as the
incarnation of God, might conceivably make any sense to us.

We might begin by reflecting on the statement: 'and the word
was made flesh and dwelt among us'.[6] This metaphor 'word
was made flesh' has been chosen by St John to describe the inde-
scribable. As a metaphor, the phrase brings together two seemingly contradictory notions, 'word' and 'flesh'. By 'word' is intended not simply the word of God as it had been understood in
the Old Testament, but 'spirit' of God, and the whole outpouring of God himself that was only begun to be grasped in the

---

5. Jn ch 18, 19.
6. Jn 1:14.

revelation of Christ. By 'flesh' is intended the fact that this out-pouring of the person of God has entered into human history in the form of a human person, that is, the man Jesus. The claim of Jesus that he is son of God, that he is in some sense God, has to be understood in all of this seeming strangeness and novelty.

Three Divine Persons

When Jesus began to indicate that God was more than had been previously supposed, that the one God was somehow Father and Son, he opened up the inner life of God to his hearers. He also spoke of God as 'Holy Spirit'. This is asserted to be a third person that dwells with Father and Son in the one and same God. In other words, God is one and God is three. It is the doctrine of the Blessed Trinity.

The ancient texts of the Old Testament had frequently spoken of the 'Spirit' of God being active in the world. The book of Genesis tells how the spirit 'hovered' over creation at the very beginning.[7] A whole selection of texts, known as the 'wisdom' literature, speaks of the 'wisdom' of God as being almost a separate person who lived and 'played with' God.[8] This person is often described in female terms. Christians recognise in these texts intimations of the incarnation of the Word, which is Jesus, and intimations of the Holy Spirit.

Jesus said to his apostles that he would send them another advocate, a comforter, who would guide them in the trials that lay ahead.[9] The Holy Spirit, the third person of the Blessed Trinity, is the name we give to this guide. Yet the term 'Holy Spirit' has to be understood as metaphor. The word 'spirit' comes from the Latin *spiro*, to breathe. It is meant to convey the idea of the breath of God moving in the world. In the original Hebrew, the breath of God, *ruah*, is something wonderful, creative and 'holy-making', and it somehow links all life to God

---

7. Gen 1:2.
8. See, for example, Introduction to the Wisdom Books, in *The Jerusalem Bible*, London 1966, pp 724-725.
9. Jn 14:26.

who creates life. We name the Holy Spirit in this way. We have no other way of describing what the Holy Spirit is other than with this strange name. These terms are symbols, rough impressions, which convey to us some minimal idea of what is being spoken about. They are not exact in the sense of legal or scientific exactness, nor are they meant to be.

Even the term '*Abba*', that unique term meaning something like our word 'Papa', that Jesus used to refer to the one who is 'Our Father', is a metaphor; its meaning is intended to be primarily symbolic. Jesus chose an image of an affectionate father to convey something of the reality of God to us and to enable us to relate to that God. It is Jesus himself, of course, who is the primary revelation of God to us. When we want to think about what God is like, what the attitudes of God are, we have only to think of Jesus.

Jesus is the Saviour
Let us now consider this question of Father, Son and Holy Spirit in the context of that other claim that has been mentioned. God has revealed that Jesus is the one who will save his people from their sins, and who will ultimately overcome the evil that is in the world. We must entertain this issue in all of its seriousness. For most people, a realisation of their own imperfection and selfishness is not in question. Many recognise, also, that the presence of evil in the world is pervasive. Whatever we call evil or however we explain it, it continues to be the single most scandalous feature in the world, scandalous enough to prevent many from believing there is, or can be, a good God.

We readily recognise the distinction that exists between innocence and guilt in human affairs. This distinction, according to those who believe, has a larger explanation than might be apparent at first. God has revealed to us that the fault we see is not only our fault; it is a fault that exists at a wider and deeper level than any of us. Yet that fault is not God's fault; it is a failing that has arisen from the very excellence of creation, namely from the gift of freedom which God wants creatures to have. It is the God-given freedom of creatures that has brought us, for better and for worse, to the world that we now know.

If the evil in this world is not the fault of God, and if it is only partially the fault of men and women, then who else might be to blame for it? Here again we can only make progress with the help of metaphor. Names like 'Satan' or 'the devil', or phrases like 'prince of darkness' or 'mystery of iniquity' have been used to designate a personage, a fallen being who has the ultimate responsibility for evil. 'Satan' and 'mystery of iniquity' are metaphoric terms for something or someone that is not God, for one who at a deeper level than humanity has already rejected God.

These metaphors are part of revelation. We need to have it confirmed for us that the evil we already know really does exist at some level that is beyond our own individual making. So often, evil seems to be embedded even in nature. By providing that confirmation of a deeper meaning to every human struggle, God invites us to entrust ourselves and those whom we love more completely to him.

So the human race is saved by the work of one who is a son of God in a very special sense. It is saved in a context where this saving or salvation is one which cannot be brought about by anyone who is simply and only a human person. There is, moreover, an important link between the idea of redemption by God and the fall of humanity, or what is often called original sin.[10]

The Christian believes that Jesus Christ, 'son of God', has already completed on earth the task of redemption by becoming a human person and by dying on Calvary. But how the life, death and resurrection of Jesus could cause humanity to be redeemed and brought back into its state of innocence with God is something that we must now examine.

---

10. Gen 3:1-24.

The idea of redemption

Notice how the discussion has moved wholly away from the 'here and now' narrative that is presented to us in the gospels. The themes of Jesus' divine identity and of the real nature of the underlying evil that is found in the world represent an important shift of perspective. We have moved from the personal and historical detail of the journeys, preaching and healing of Jesus to matters that have to do with the more profound reaches of belief. From this new perspective, everything is more speculative. For that very reason, we are more prone to err on this ground. The history of theology reminds us of many false starts and abandoned theories, not to mention the danger of heresy.

I begin by setting out the basic points of my theological compass. It has been revealed that this world is good, as it has issued from the hand of God. But revelation has also confirmed that the world is 'fallen', and hence the purpose of creation has been in some sense defeated. This idea corresponds with a basic perception that exists in many of us that, for all its goodness, the world is very corrupt.

The world is, furthermore, a place of flesh and blood. It is the material, ordinary world that we know. It consists of body as well as soul. To be saved, the world would need to be redeemed through and through. The very ordinariness, the sense of 'down to earth' that is so important to a real grasp of things, would need to be 'saved'.

This too is what we find in the gospels. The language of redemption completely transforms the ordinary day to day life of this world when it puts that existence into the much wider context of eternal life. This language refers not only to the real world of now, as we know it; it refers also to the world that awaits us when we die, the detail of which we have no idea. This transformation of perspective is one that includes the whole of creation, earth and heaven as well. It touches everything that is.

There have been many exaggerations of redemption theory. Perhaps the most familiar of these is that which polarises God the Father and God the Son. It suggests that in order to appease the anger of God the Father, God the Son took the place of sinful men and women and underwent death on the cross. In other words, Jesus somehow persuaded God the Father to admit the human race to redemption. What is true in this theory lies in the identification of Jesus with sinful humanity, but this truth comes at the expense of a total distortion of God the Father.[11]

While we must recognise that the faith of many Christians has rested on theories of this kind, we are not required to subscribe to such theories. They do not seem today to square ultimately with our sense of the God of revelation.

Yet this very polarising exaggeration may suggest a way of looking at things that has relevance in our own day. We need an image of Jesus and of his heavenly Father with which it is possible to identify in order to understand more fully what has been done for us. If we turn to the pages of the Letter to the Hebrews again, we read there these words:

Therefore he had to be made like his brethren in every respect, so that he might become a merciful and faithful high priest in the service of God, to make expiation for the sins of the people. For because he himself has suffered and been tempted, he is able to help those who are tempted.[12]

It is useful to stand back from the theological mindset that frames this text, by which I mean the terms 'high priest', 'expiation' and 'sacrifice'. In doing so, we see that the dominant idea is that of the identification of Christ with the actual people of God and, by extension, all the people of the earth. When we say that Jesus identifies with the people of God, we are also saying that God identifies with his people. In loving us, God, in the person of Jesus, becomes one of us and, in drawing us to himself, God submits to a humiliation and death that cannot fail to convince us of his identification with humankind. This makes it more possible to see why the cross is such a powerful symbol.

---

11. Even St Thomas' association of this theory with divine justice seems to prevent it, in our eyes, from ultimately resting in God's mercy, where St Thomas locates it; *Summa Theologica*, 111, q 46, ad 3.
12. Heb 2:17-18.

With metaphor, we may retain the language of sacrifice, and retain the language of sharing in the sacrifice by eating it and drinking it. Moreover, it permits us to stay always within the limitations of our own flesh and blood. That is, to stay with suffering and grief as basic elements of our experience in the world. God has given us the passion and death of Christ, and the meanings that go with it, as a vital form of identification with what we are. This happens to be very much a part of human reality: we overlook or 'phase out' those aspects of reality that we do not wish to see. With God, there is no rationalisation, no phasing out of our real state. By identifying with us in a free act on his part, Jesus shows us how completely human he has become, how completely humanity has been redeemed and loved by him. No suffering is outside of his suffering. It is as if God is saying to us: look at suffering, look at pain, look at flesh and blood, look at all that is real in the world. This too is very much a part of human reality. In Peter's first letter we read:

Remember, the ransom that was paid to free you ... the precious blood of a lamb without spot or stain, namely Christ ... [13]

In the passion and death of Christ we are also speaking, in a sense, of metaphor. By speaking of the death of a lamb, namely Christ, as metaphor, I do not wish to minimise the agony that was involved in that death. It was of course the darkest night, where even the protection and the will of the Father were invisible to him.

Now, perhaps, we can understand more clearly and more fully when the psalmist says: 'the Lord is near to the broken hearted; and saves the crushed in spirit'.[14] An impression of God is emerging that is not only wholly unexpected, humanly speaking, but that goes against the grain of our normal expectations of an all-powerful figure.

The God of revelation, as shown in Jesus, is contrary to every selfish and violent choice against others that is made. He stands unswervingly for the unifying of every man and woman in him.

13. 1 Pet 18:21.
14. Ps 33:18.

But that opposition to selfishness and to violence constitutes what we might call a great strength in God, as does his unswerving will for the unifying of all persons with him. When God is revealed in Jesus Christ, what we see is his immense moral strength, courage and conviction. He is marked by his compassion for all who suffer.

And so we have a view of Jesus as saviour who is an example to us of what God really is. Being God, he takes up his position as the humblest human being from what we may suppose to be the distant perfection of heaven.[15] Into this world of the downtrodden, Jesus comes, vulnerable and humble. He takes up the cause of humanity in the context of the 'humble of the earth'. Yet we do to him what we have done already, or what has been done already in our name, to countless of his creatures, to countless of our brothers and sisters. He dies a lonely and a truly terrible death at the hands of others. In this way, it is even we ourselves who have 'validated' his life and his death as redemptive by persecuting him. We have proved the prophets true. Jesus has entered the arena of this world freely and, although he is the one 'who is without sin', he is now the one who 'has become sin', as St Paul puts it.[16]

The Resurrection of Jesus
And God raised him 'on the third day'. The resurrection of Christ has been, of course, a scandal[17] since the New Testament itself. In Mark's version, the women who visited the tomb to find it empty are recorded as being amazed.[18] In John's account, we are told, Jesus appeared to Mary Magdalene and she did not at first recognise him.[19] Nor did the disciples recognise him on

---

15. Phil 2:1-11.
16. 2 Cor 5:21: *'God made the sinless one into sin, so that in him we might become the goodness of God.'*
17. On Christ as scandal, see Xavier Leon-Dufour, op. cit., Scandal, p 463-4.
18. Mk 16:5.
19. Jn 20:14-18.

the road to Emmaus.[20] Later again, we are told that, on two occasions, the apostles refused to believe those who had seen Jesus risen.[21] The apostle Thomas is quoted as saying: 'Unless I see in his hands the print of the nails, and place my finger in the mark of the nails, and place my hand in his side, I will not believe'.[22] In the Acts of the Apostles, on hearing that God had raised someone from the dead, the men of Athens dismiss Paul with the words: 'We will hear you again about this.'[23]

The resurrection of Jesus and the resurrection of the human body are central to the Christian faith. It was Paul who wrote: 'If Christ has not been raised, then our preaching is in vain and your faith is in vain.'[24] We might say that belief in Christ demands something like his resurrection from the dead.

It appears that the risen human body can be shown to us in some recognisable way. At least, Jesus showed himself on several occasions to many different people. Paul refers to an appearance of Christ to more than five hundred people at the same time, most of whom are still alive, though some have died'.[25] And the risen body can bear the marks of wounds that have been suffered. Jesus said to Thomas, not without humour one may suspect, some eight days after the apostle's refusal to believe the witness of the others, 'Put your finger here and see my hands; and put out your hand, and place it in my side; do not be faithless but believing.'[26]

When we say that God raises us from the dead, we mean to assert that it is the whole person that is raised to a new life. But this new life is not at all the same as the life that we live now. It is possible to believe on God's word that human life exists in some

20. Lk 24 13-35.
21. Mk 16:9-15.
22. Jn 20:25.
23. Acts 17:32-33.
24. 1 Cor 15:13-14.
25. 1 Cor 15:6.
26. Jn 20:27.

new form after death, although we have very little idea of what that life is like.[27]

An explanation in theology seeks only to provide a way of taking hold of something that is intellectually beyond our complete grasp. We live in an age that demands to know how everything 'works'. That is an aspect of human rationality that is at once something wonderful and yet limited. Ultimately, how redemption works is beyond our knowing. We know of these things because God has revealed them to us. A theory of redemption seeks only to bring together the person of Jesus with our own experience of being in the world, and to bring them together in a way that seeks to reflect as truthfully as possible what has been revealed.

Theology seeks to make sense of what we have been told. That God could be anything like his portrayal in revelation is truly amazing. Many of our contemporaries, we know, reject these ideas out of hand as mere fantasy. This fantasy is translated very quickly into a kind of fairy tale fantasy. For the believer, on the other hand, this is the whole picture that makes sense of or gives meaning to creation. In this account, within this belief scheme or interpretation, everything is transformed: God, humanity and the world. For the believer, theology makes sense, not fantasy, of reality.

27. See, for example, Karl Rahner SJ, 'The Resurrection Of The Body', *Theological Investigations* vol 2 (London 1963), and 'What Does It Mean Today To Believe In Jesus Christ?' *Theological Investigations* vol 18 (London 1984).

CHAPTER EIGHT

Faith, Motivation and Communication with God

Anyone who reads Homer's epic poem 'The Iliad' cannot but be struck by the amount of text that is taken up with putting heart into the warriors of Greece and Troy. The siege of Troy supposedly dragged on for seven long years. Clearly the importance of putting motivation into the hearts of the leaders and the troops was a major task.

In the gospel of Matthew, Jesus is approached by a leper who asks to be healed: '"Lord, if you will, you can make me clean." And he stretched out his hand and touched him, saying, "I will; be clean." And immediately his leprosy was cleansed.'[1] This incident touches on the motivation of Jesus and on the motivation of the leper. It shows that sense of 'wanting to' that is an essential dimension of faith. In the gospel of St John, after the resurrection, Jesus asks Peter three times whether he (Peter) loves him.[2] Here it is evident that the motivation of Peter is being tested following his earlier three-fold denial of Jesus during the passion.

The question of motivation, or wanting to, affects not only belief. It can affect unbelief as well. People may withhold belief, not simply because they are indifferent to it, but because they do not want to believe.

Wanting to believe

The role of the will in the act of faith cropped up explicitly in three of the interviews that took place in the context of this book. There was one person, just on the edges of our talk, who indi-

1. Mt 8:2-3; see also Mk 1:40-45; Lk 5:12-13.
2. Jn 21:15-17.

rectly threw a particular light on the importance of human volition. This was Paula's husband, Don, who was minding the
baby in the next room during our conversation. Don had been
brought up by his family to be an agnostic. Paula was very sure
that was something she would never want to be. Once again her
wish is expressed in concrete terms, as exemplified in the difference between herself and her husband on this point:

*Don's father is actually an atheist, he doesn't believe. He believes
that when you are in the ground that's it, finished. When Mr B dies
… he doesn't want anything, he doesn't want to go to the church. I
mean there's no place really even for anybody to say goodbye.
That's it, and he thinks that that's it; he is never going to meet anybody again. And I'd hate, I'd hate even my children to think that. I
think … I know, I hope I know, that when I die, and I go up there,
please God, if I get up there, that I can look after everybody around
here. In other words, they say the soul goes to heaven. This is just
the skeleton, and that gets buried, but when I go up there, I can look
after everybody … and that I have somewhere else to go. What is life
all about then if it's just to be put here on the earth and do whatever
it is that you have to do, and that's it then, that's the finish of the
whole lot of it. That's just the way I feel.*

The implications of Paula's belief for her actual way of life
are felt very deeply:

*I always say Don is agnostic, he's sitting on a fence, he doesn't
know which side he is on. The time that Don's mother died, I said to
him: 'If it was my mother or father, I'd go up and light a candle in
the church … I'd ask people to say a prayer for my Mam, but you
have nothing.' He comes to Mass with us at Christmas, and that's
the only time I ask him to come to Mass with us.*

There is a huge sense of Paula's wanting to believe, in this
passage. It is almost as if the desire to believe were enough to
sustain the belief.

Declan was very certain, however, that he did not believe
and that he did not want to believe in any kind of God at all. He
and I explored this idea of volition in faith a little further: 'Some

people believe, it is said, because they want to believe. Others do not believe because they do not want to believe. Would you agree?'

I think people believe because they want to believe. I think there is a huge compulsion within the human being to want to believe. I think there is a huge impulse in the human to believe in something ... that has been moved to believe in something. I think there is that need to believe in something. Now why should that be there? Is there some deficiency in us? Or is there some huge advantage to us ... would we be the supreme animals that we are today if it wasn't there? I don't know, and I haven't been impelled, quite frankly, to go and find out. For a time, and it was put to me, I was told I was posturing ... you know, 'act the hard man, act the radical, professional atheist' ... this kind of thing. And I did wonder if I really was doing it just to create an impression. I don't think I am, because for various reasons I don't move much in society, I don't very often have to justify my positions or beliefs to anybody except myself ... and I have no difficulty ... not even in trying to impress myself! (Laughing)

My reply was not as he had anticipated: 'I wonder how important it is that we want to believe, or to disbelieve ...'

Do you think you can want to disbelieve ... it hadn't occurred to me, quite honestly, that one might want to disbelieve ... short-sightedness on my part ...

'Well, I think it is possible ... if it is possible to want to believe, then it must be possible to want to disbelieve. It could be that a person's perception of God is so injurious that he or she might say: "I couldn't believe in that ..." and so "I don't want to believe in that ..." Or equally a person might have such a view of life, shall we say, that he or she might say: "I wouldn't last a minute without God, I really want to believe ..." I think the "wanting" has a role to play ...'

I wonder what the motivation would be, when you say 'I want not to believe'? Obviously the motivation for wanting to believe is very clear-cut, as I understood it anyway. There is a reward for believing.

*I am thinking now perhaps in the traditional religious way ... that
if you do believe and behave correctly, you are rewarded. Whereas,
what is the reward of disbelieving?*

Our discussion continued briefly on the idea of reward. I asserted: 'When I say "wanting to" I wasn't so much thinking of
reward, but of the way people say "I do want to know the truth
... I really want to know ..." "Wanting" in that sense ...'

*Yes. You use the expression 'the truth' as though there is an answer
to which one can progress through ultimately.*

My own impression of truth as something that is identifiable
in part and nameable is one that Declan would want to question.

At this point Declan introduced a topic that he felt very
strongly about concerning his early religious formation as a
child:

*Unless it is a very negative thing, it is a bit of a reactionary thing;
which is quite likely, because I did suffer a very severe reaction
against being conned in my young life. I was quite bitter about it,
quite honestly ... about having been imbued with evil ... with a
sense of evil. If there is one thing I will not forgive the church for ...*
(Declan is quite angry at this point) *quite honestly, it is imbuing
small children with a sense of evil ... I mean ... it was practically the
first thing. And if you're correct, there is a 'wanting not to believe',
and if there is a motivation ... I never thought of it like that ... but,
my outrage, quite frankly, when my life was at its most formative
stage ... the 'formative' stage never changes ... that you are imbued
with a sense of evil, that you can be an agent of evil ... an innocent
agent of evil, if that is not a contradiction in terms ... I cannot forgive the church. I do hope these days that children being brought up
are not being presented with 'original sin' as the first concept they
come to ... which I think is a most appalling thing to do to children.*

Declan insisted, however, that his recollection of loss of belief
was more an intellectual exercise than a reactive one.

My conversation with Martin on this point of motivation
took a somewhat different direction. Martin spoke passionately
about trusting in God whatever the circumstances of one's life,

so much so that I am reminded of the ancient speakers in Homer rousing up their men when they had thought that all was lost:

> *And the one thing which strikes me more than anything else over the years is the value of prayer, in the sense that people can get anything they want ... and I say that deliberately ... anything they want by praying. Now, because people do not get an immediate answer to prayer, they say: 'Ah, that's for the birds, nothing happened.' Nothing does happen for a long, long time, and in some cases it may not happen for years ... but it does happen, for the very reason that you have to keep on reminding the Lord that he promised and that he cannot break his promise. He said: 'Anything you ask in my name, he will give it to you, my father will give it to you.' And the greatest act of faith of all is when he says 'Anything you ask, believing that you have received ... anything you ask, believing that you have received it.' That is an extraordinary thing, 'believing that you have received it, it shall be done unto you'. In other words, if you have that great leap of faith that takes you across the divide from a no belief or a half belief situation to a situation where you ask for something 'believing that you have received it', the favour has already been granted. If you can make that jump of faith, then your pain, your request is granted. But as I say, and I keep telling people this, and I feel almost aggressive about it at times because I say 'this is what he said ... and you have got to take him at his word, and you have got to demand it; you're not going in saying "Now please Lord help me." You have to demand it. This is what he said ... so remember it.'*

Martin's faith is quite concrete and focused in this passage where he speaks about prayer. It is clear that he, too, believes because he wants to believe.

In the case of Suzanne, however, the 'wanting' element is not mentioned yet I suggest that it is there. Suzanne feels the need for order in society and for values. In a sense this stems naturally from her sociological outlook. She finds it difficult to contemplate the anarchic situations in which some children have to grow up. In fact, it is her role as a parent that informs much of

her thinking at these levels. I had put it to her that she was attracted mostly to the values aspect of religion:

> *Well it attracts me, it attracts me in the sense that I think commu-
> nity needs order and needs structure. You can get back to Marx and
> the 'opium of the people', and all that. I would in my twenties have
> said: 'Oh it's a form of social control', and rejected religion that
> way, and everything else ... now I would probably say: 'Yes it is a
> form of social control and that's a good thing.'*

I had mentioned to Suzanne the feeling of well being that is
often encountered in association with religious thought. This led
her to wonder about a force within us to have a good life:

> *I was just thinking there, as you were talking, just thinking aloud
> again. I suppose the accepted wisdom is that God is something out
> there, beyond the clouds, that it is one being, embracing all of us. I
> don't know that this is a philosophical thought, in any fashion any-
> where, already thought through. Supposing that it's actually some-
> where within yourself, that there's a God inside all of us ... because
> you see there is a force within us to live a good life. The natural
> human condition is to live and is to help others live, so that does
> come from somewhere. Is it just part of our make up as humans, the
> way the stem is part of the daffodil, or is it something more than
> that? That's what is interesting ... because it is natural, even where
> atrocities have happened in the world. It is people operating within a
> sphere where they do actually think they are doing the right thing.
> It's some kind of flaw, I forget the genetic term, but its like you get a
> bad strain of daffodils, something went awry, and then it corrects ...*

There is something like a concept of volition here, an idea of
belief being desirable, wanted, but it is as yet very vague.
Suzanne is a contented person. She is happy to describe herself
as an agnostic, but she recognises that there is a value to having
thought things out.

> *It wouldn't bother me. I wouldn't have strong views either. I re-
> spect people who believe what they believe, because there's nothing
> to say that anybody's view of the world is more valid than anybody
> else's, because we just don't know ... we just don't know. And, if*

people choose to believe in a particular interpretation, I would have a certain amount of envy for them. It's good to have a shape on your thoughts ... it's good to get to that stage. I think its good to have thought it through. I think a lot of people are very accepting ... just as I am accepting. I accept life. So I don't get into major questions. Maybe my equal is somebody who completely accepts the church and the stories and the scriptures and everything else, and the end effect on their life is the same as mine. You want to live a good life and get on with things.

I said to Suzanne that she had been consistent all the way through our conversation, and that it had been difficult to pin her down on whether or not she really wanted to believe. I suggested to her that she would agree that there was a morality, but that it was simply a social morality:

You are reminding me of the whole nurture/nature debate. I think definitely society is made up of individuals who have a nature ... and maybe that brings us back to evil. Maybe some people just do have a nature that is never going to come within the social agreement. So maybe what society is ... it's a common understanding of how a whole set of individuals are going to behave. And individuals do come from different starting points ... back to what we said at the very beginning, your intellect, or your way of thinking. There's something in us that's more than the cells, and bone ... other than our body. Morality is such a long piece of string ...

This brought us to the idea of the church as a force for good in society, as an institution that provided order and a kind of parenting that seems now to be lacking:

The kind of group we've been talking about who don't see the church in the parental kind of role, well, where is that parental role? Where is it on the kind of issues we have been talking about, let us say contraception, or teenage pregnancy, or divorce, or whether one is straight or gay? Who supplies the values? Is it more in the workplace, maybe some kind of organisational belonging there? I don't think so, actually. I might have said that a few years ago. I don't know where it is. Do people get it from their partners and their rela-

tionships? Or are relationships different now? Where relationships are good are they stronger and communicating more, and maybe people expect more and maybe that's why there's more divorce. People of my generation would expect far more from a marriage in terms of communication and understanding than my parents would have, where it was a structure you went into. So then maybe they needed something else ...

Suzanne does not come across as having a strong active desire to believe. I attempted to put into words what it actually meant for Suzanne to call herself Catholic:

'How might we describe what it means for you to be what you are? In a general sociological sense you put your hand up to being a Catholic, but in a very broad sense, to respecting some of the values that are upheld by Catholicism, but definitely not others ... a broad support for general values which are upheld by common consent shall we say, in the sense that a person of any denomination or of none might subscribe to societal values; to be a Catholic because one was born a Catholic but not too much more than that ... "While my parents are Catholic, and I respect them very much, and would not wish to offend them, we do not really agree on the issue of Catholicism ..." How am I doing?'

I think you are summing it up; you're summing it up fairly correctly. I think too, though, there was a journey in getting to here as well. I think there would have been times when I would have been quite angry with the church ... the church's position on things, the church's view, as I might have perceived it, which might have been wrong. It might be the church's view of the place of women in society, the place of women in the church. Certainly as a younger woman, yes, I would have been very angry. And I think, maybe, I have reached an accommodation that I'm not going to let the things that make me angry ... end up with me rejecting the package. I'm going to live and let live.

Suzanne articulates a number of inhibitions to motivation to belief that are shared by many women and men.

Now, I suppose, in terms of where I want to be ... I often feel I don't

*know enough ... actually. I would like to know more about, say, the
church's view on women in the church, because I know, I suspect, it
is not anything like as simplistic as we see it. Except the way we all
see it is the way that it is ... perception is the reality at the end of the
day. When I was a young girl ... the idea of female altar boys, altar
girls, would have definitely been a non-runner. Now I'm not sure I
ever consciously wanted to be an altar girl, but gosh if you are excluded, it's a very different kettle of fish. I am quite sure I never as-
pired to being a priest, but I might have felt that it was something
that should have been open to me.*

As she continued, Suzanne shows how aspects of the institution of the Catholic Church alienates her:

*Now at this stage I'd be inclined to say that the church is going to
have to wise up and have women priests ... or there won't be a
church. From a logistical numbers point of view ... there may be
economic reasons about priests not marrying, or women not being
in the church. As a woman there would be a certain degree of exclu-
sion ... it's a boy's club ... it's very much a boy's club* (laughter).
*And it's a bit like ... 'You can be an associate member'. But having
said that, I haven't bothered particularly to get involved ... and
women can get involved, but you do suspect that there is a certain
amount of tokenism there. I think it is still a patriarchy ...*

'At the back of your mind there may be a judgement: this is
how men are. And you are reading this into your judgement of
the church?' I asked, to which she replied:

*Yes. If you take it in the workplace ... the dynamic of a meeting
which is mixed ... men and women ... and a meeting which is all
male ... it's a completely different dynamic, and it's the mix that
brings the quality ... all female is just as bad. It's the mix that
brings the quality to thinking and decision-making. That would
have angered me about the church, but I probably don't care enough
for it to anger me at the moment ... and maybe that's deliberate as
well. I remember being at Mass one day with the two kids, and
Rosa, who was then about four, said very loudly at one of the very
quiet, contemplative times during the ceremony: 'Mammy can I be*

*a priest when I grow up ...' She liked the idea of being up there ...
and, you know, the reality is, if she was a boy, gosh lots of people ...
grandparents would be thrilled ... that's exaggerating but, yes, if
she were a boy ... there's a role model there, there's a society that
you can identify with. And as a girl it starts at that very early age,
'well that's a club for other people.' That's one angle ... and while
there are structures for women in the church, they haven't succeed-
ed in making that work. So I think that's a pity. But I spend my
whole working life in a male world as well ... and I survive it ...*

This has been a long excursion into Suzanne's views on religious matters. Of the four conversations, it is ambivalent on the
issue of 'wanting to believe'. Yet, there is enough, even here, to
justify the assertion that motivation or volition is important in
every case. Suzanne has experienced disappointment and frustration in her religious experience, yet she appears to be willing
to keep giving it a try. She does not want to throw away the
whole package; there is something there that continues to draw
her, although she finds it difficult to name exactly what that
something is: *'your intellect, or your way of thinking ... there's something in us that's more than the cells and bone ... other than our body'.*
I think that Suzanne's position is very similar to that of many
people today.

Wanting to understand – support for faith
The question of motivation arises for all knowledge, whether
secular or religious. 'I believe that I may understand,' Anselm
said. The motivation to understand is the one that moves all
people who study. Any person who seeks the truth of some
question, any question, is motivated by the desire to know. We
do not come to knowledge through personal indifference. We
have to reckon with that hidden motivation that lies behind all
knowledge and that acts as a spring that releases the mind into
what might be called a fruitful cycle.

Associated with this question of motivation is the problem of
searching for the truth if there is no hope of reaching it. Why
should there be a thirst for some kind of ultimate understanding,

if there is nothing to be understood at this level? It is not enough to state that there will always be a superabundance of secular knowledge to keep the minds of people occupied. The fact is that there still exist more ultimate questions that also require some kind of response. The plays of Samuel Beckett speak to a society that knows the frustration of not knowing answers to ultimate questions. Newman put the matter more positively. He was convinced that hunger for the truth was one of the great witnesses to the existence of truth.[3]

Certain human motivations are a suggestion, a warranty even, that there is some corresponding value that can meet them. I believe that the motivation that seeks to believe in God is a motivation that can be understood in this way.

For Martin, faith is about saying yes and wanting to say yes to all that is good. For him, faith is about what is assumed to be the case unless the contrary is shown. And in the case of Christian belief, the contrary cannot be shown. As Martin sees it, faith is a practical matter for ordinary people in everyday life, and it requires only the most practical everyday judgements, as does everything else that a person normally does.

Communication with God

Christian faith, as we have said earlier, is always initiated by God. The motivation to believe, that is, the personal experience of 'wanting to believe', of being drawn towards belief, is a response to this gift. The person who is motivated to believe that there is a God and, moreover, that this God is in communication with him or her is not alone in the world in his or her convictions.

It is evident that human beings of every kind say that they do know and communicate with God. It is clear that they have done so for thousands of years. Many people, whose intelligence and judgement are respected in other matters, are confidently in touch with God each day, some of them despite the most difficult personal circumstances. For them, a form of communication

---

3. *Historical Sketches*, (London 1872-3) vol I, p 165.

already exists, a communication that creates the possibility that the simplest person, even a child, might understand and respond emotionally and naturally to God.

People of every continent, of every race and of every culture believe that they are more or less in touch with a being that they call God, even though they envisage or imagine that being differently from the way that Christians do. They express a deep sentiment of humanity that goes back to the dawn of time. As believers, we recognise that we are members of one human family.[4] The fact that this belief exists, and that it has existed for a very long time, ought not to be overlooked. This fact of belief, while not a proof of God's existence, does represent some kind of probability that ought to be considered on its own terms.[5] People do not require 'proof', as such, for what is normal; proof is always the exception in ordinary human affairs.[6] Proof has to be exact, deliberate, beyond all reasonable doubt. This is not the way of ordinary life. If ordinary life were like this, it would grind to a standstill.

While Declan has no belief whatsoever in God, he does freely acknowledge the backwardness and ignorance that is present in the human community.

So, if I understand your question correctly, I'm interested in something more than I see around me. Certainly if I look at society, as I see it, God forgive me using this expression: there has to be more than this. I love life. I think humankind is a disaster at the moment. I think our system, our social system, our financial systems are a disaster. I think our society is based on greed and aggression ... even the parts of it held up for most acclaim, even democracy sounds

---

4. For Newman's view of 'natural religion' – and this includes the basic distinction between right and wrong – see *University Sermons*, op. cit., II, 'The Influence of Natural and Revealed Religion respectively', pp 16ff.
5. For a discussion on the idea of Antecedent Probability, see Robin C. Selby, *The Principle of Reserve in the Writings of John Henry Cardinal Newman*, Oxford, 1975, pp 75-88.
6. *Grammar of Assent*, op.cit., p 618-23; see also *University Sermons*, op. cit., Sermon X, Faith and Reason, contrasted as habits of mind, pp 176-201, esp p 184-5; see Ian Ker, *John Henry Newman, a biography*, Oxford 1990, pp 211, 645, for discussion of this point.

vulnerable when you get down to it. I think that what he (humankind) *is managing to do with the planet is unforgivable ... stupid
in the extreme. He is so greedy and so short-sighted that ... again I
come back to the point ... if this is humanity ... if this is the peak of
creation ... God help us. God isn't there to help us, but let us help
ourselves before it is too late ... let our stupidity be apparent. I have
no firm belief that we will. You might say: 'Surely our spiritual dimension, our religion, whatever, should bring us back.' I can't see
any evidence that they are even trying to bring us back ... and I
would despair of the future, quite frankly.*

Once again, I have to state that I am not bringing forward a
proof of anything. I am trying simply to look at the world as it is
and to listen to it as objectively as I can. In that listening, I hear a
comprehensible call on the part of ordinary people for an intelligent and a more selfless approach that will help us to put everything more to rights. Indeed, the approach of Declan is, itself,
evidence of such a call.

The novel *Callista*, set in North Africa in the third century AD,
tells the story of a fictional heroine who is, ultimately, martyred
for her faith. The following words are addressed to a questioning Callista by a Christian:

'*... if all your thoughts go one way; if you have needs, desires, aims,
aspirations, all of which demand an Object, and imply, by their
very existence, that such an Object does exist also; and if nothing
here does satisfy them, and if there be a message which professes to
come from that Object, of whom you already have the presentiment,
and to teach you about Him, and to bring you the remedy you
crave; and if those who try that remedy say with one voice that the
remedy answers; are you not bound, Callista, at least to look that
way, to inquire into what you hear about it, and to ask for His help,
if He be, to enable you to believe in Him?*'[6]

6. *Callista, A Sketch of the Third Century,* (London 1873) p 220. The fictional Christian who puts the question to Callista is based on the person
of St Cyprian, a presbyter and bishop in contemporary North Africa,
and also a martyr.

This question is a valid one. It is a natural, normal, human question. It is a question that puts us in touch with some kind of basic human motivation. That is all that my argument seeks to show. There is a real need, identified by many; and we have, close at hand, a faith that answers this need to an infinite degree.

The fact that, in the human heart, there can be a desire for God could be an indication that God actually exists. Such desire is not a proof.[7] Nothing definite can be concluded from it alone. When grasped, however, by the ordinary mind, it is capable of showing with clarity that there could be a supernatural dimension present to the universe. For believers, this possibility leads on to faith.

---

7. Selby, op. cit., p 88. There can be a sequence of thoughts or considerations that may convince oneself or others about a situation or state of affairs that may exist.

CHAPTER NINE

An Invitation to the Gospel

As we have seen, 'Revelation' is a phased, gradual disclosure about God, the world and humanity that began with the prophet Abraham and that reached its climax in the life, death and resurrection of Jesus Christ. An important aspect of revelation, but not the most important aspect, is its reasonableness. We can see this very clearly in the 'Covenant' and the 'Ten Commandments'.

We find the story of the 'Covenant' between God and Israel in the books of Exodus and Deuteronomy in the Bible.[1] These books tell of the events surrounding the leaving of Egypt by the people of Israel under the leadership of Moses, about 1500 BC, and the people's entry into the Promised Land. Scholars tell us, however, that variations on the 'Ten Commandments' appear in morality found in many religions of the Near East.[2] The commandments are a common link between many ancient religions.

The commandments are animated by a sense of God and a sense of justice and fair play. If you look at the last seven of them carefully, those that apply to our relationships with each other, you will see the very human injunction with which all children are familiar: 'Be Fair.' We could add that they are sustained also by an enlightened sense of self-interest. For people who live in community and who practise the virtues of neighbourliness, this is what we would have anticipated. In this sense, the commandments are essential and they are obvious.

What characterises revelation, however, is not simply its rationality. There is an overall imaginative thrust that appeals to

---

1. Ex 20:2-17; Deut 5:6-21 & par.
2. See for example Xavier Leon Dufour SJ, op. cit., art. 'Covenant', pp 75-77.

a world order that is different to the one with which we are familiar. This alternative world order is one that challenges us at every turn. When we think about it, we begin to realise, I believe, that it is this imaginative awareness of alternative existences or scenarios, and not reasonableness simply, that is the starting point of a Christian life. How does a person live this imaginative awareness, how does one transcend rationality in one's own existence? These are the themes of this chapter.

The Good News

The story of the passion of Jesus and his death on the cross offers everybody a new and most unlikely way of interpreting their own existence. Listening to the word of revelation, we no longer look only to a 'possible' God of nature, or to a 'rational' God. We contemplate, rather, the 'actual' God who has become human like us, and whose tragic yet glorious life on earth has become a template of humanity.

Seen in the light of revelation, the story of Jesus is one that is capable of including in its detail every person who has ever lived. Themes like vocation and struggle, grace and guilt, love and hatred, success and failure, characterise this story.

The teaching of Jesus involves many sayings, attitudes, parables and deeds. Chance encounters, like that of the widow putting her few pence into the treasury at Jerusalem,[3] or the woman who washed his feet and dried them with her hair,[4] or his response to the paralytic man who was let down through the roof to be healed by him,[5] all of these prompted unexpected observations from him that were profound and totally transformed the imaginative landscape in which the everyday life of people was lived. The poor widow was seen as having given everything that she had, as opposed to a paltry sum; the woman who washed his feet was seen as having loved much because she had accepted forgiveness for so much; the paralytic man re-

---

3. Mk 12:41-44 & par.
4. Lk 7:36-50.
5. Lk 5:17-26 & par.

ceived, totally unexpectedly, the forgiveness and acceptance of God. Only then was he healed. All of these ideas are beyond the scope of reasonableness as commonly accepted today. These ideas point up the 'good news' that is signified by the very word 'gospel'.

Sometimes we see the disciples taken aback by the strict or radical elements of what Jesus says. We might consider the apostle Peter's question 'Where will we go?' These words were spoken when it was evident that none of the apostles could understand what Jesus meant by saying that he would give people his flesh to eat. Yet, Peter went on to say: 'We have believed, and have come to know, that you are the Holy One of God.'[6] In other words, following Peter's thought, 'While we do not know the whole truth of this matter and probably cannot know it now, we trust you and believe in you.'

This happens also with the teaching on marriage and divorce. This is Jesus speaking: 'Have you not read that he who made them from the beginning made them male and female, and said, "For this reason a man shall leave his father and mother and be joined to his wife, and the two shall become one." What therefore God has joined together, let no man put asunder.'[7] At one level we can see at once the force and validity of this teaching. What lovers would not? Yet we can be tempted to walk away from this when we contemplate the difficulties that so many encounter in marriage. In marriage, we can see how the ideal of holiness places us in a situation of even greater responsibility than that of mere reasonableness.

As we might have expected, the moral teaching of Jesus follows on from, and deepens further, what we know from the commandments. Jesus does not add new commandments as such; rather he draws out a little further those that already exist. His moral teaching brings a new intensity to the understanding of humankind that had been received and treasured by the Jews.

Hence, in response to the question that was put by the lawyer

6. Jn 6:69.
7. Mt 19:4-6; Gen 1:27; 2:24; Eph 5:21 & par.

to Jesus about which was the greatest commandment, Jesus replied: 'You shall love the Lord your God with all your heart, and with all your soul, and with all your mind. This is the greatest and the first commandment. And a second is like it, you shall love your neighbour as yourself. On these two commandments depend all the law and the prophets.'[8] Another version of the teaching of Jesus is the so-called golden rule: 'So whatever you wish that men and women would do to you, do so to them; for this is the law and the prophets.'[9] The different parts of Jesus' 'greatest commandment', that is the reference to God first and then the neighbour, come originally from the ancient book of Deuteronomy,[10] and they would have been very familiar to his listeners.

When we compare the commandments of the Old Testament with these teachings of Jesus, we see that there is a certain match between them, but yet there is also a difference. They seem to fit exactly and yet one exceeds the other, whether it is in relation to God, or parents, or neighbour, or family, or property, or truth telling. The new commandment of Jesus transcends completely what had been there already, yet without displacing anything essential.

A further observation on this theme would be to distinguish between different stages or categories of moral responsibility. The prophet Isaiah suggests that it is through a sense of neighbourliness and care for the weak and defenceless that men and women will find their way back to God. He has this to say about human sinfulness and divine providence:

Wash yourselves; make yourselves clean; remove the evil of your doings from before my eyes; cease to do evil and learn to do good; seek justice, correct oppression; defend the fatherless, plead for the widow.

Come now, let us reason together, says the Lord: though your sins are like scarlet, they shall be as white as snow; though they are

---

8. Mt 22:35-40 & par.
9. Mt 7:12.
10. Deut 6:4-9.

*red like crimson, they shall become like wool. If you are willing and
obedient, you shall eat the good of the land; but if you refuse and
rebel, you shall be devoured by the sword; for the mouth of the Lord
has spoken.*[11]

We find this same message in the New Testament. In his
parable setting out what the last judgement would be like, Jesus
tells us that we will be judged on a series of very concrete and
practical responses to others in need: 'For I was hungry and you
gave me food, I was thirsty and you gave me drink, I was a
stranger and you welcomed me, I was sick and you visited me, I
was in prison and you came to see me ...' And he tells us that
people will say: 'Lord, when did we see thee hungry and feed
thee ...' He then provides the unexpected reply: 'And the King
will answer them, "Truly I say to you, as you did it to one of the
least of these my brethren, you did it to me".'[12]

It is true that the Old Testament has different moral strands,
some very ancient and very different from what came to be
recognised by Jesus as the norm. We know that in the Bible there
is much hatred, war and bloodshed in the name of religion. Yet
what Jesus said was: 'Love your enemy ...' He draws on the
most profound insights of his tradition and develops them,
while he leaves behind much that was not relevant to his message: 'You have heard it said "an eye for an eye and a tooth for a
tooth," but I say unto you: "offer the wicked man no resistance.
On the contrary, if anyone hits you on the right cheek, offer him
the other as well" ...'[13]

The disciple of Christ hears the invitation of Jesus to follow
him. Whether this call is heard in radical terms: 'If you would be
perfect, go, sell what you possess and give to the poor, and you
will have treasure in heaven; then come, follow me.'[14] Or it may
be heard in more simple terms as: 'Blessed rather are those who
hear the word of God in their hearts and keep it.'[15] But it is this

11. Is 1:16-20
12. Mt 25:31-46.
13. Mt 5:38-39.
14. Mt 19:21 & par.
15. Lk 11:28 & par.

'hearing' that marks every disciple. These words echo within and cause us eventually to respond to them. Christians believe, moreover, that in moments of moral opportunity, or moral trial, or moral uncertainty, they can hear, or sense, or understand somehow, that Jesus is present to them in their hearts, urging them forward, encouraging them. It is faith that sustains this momentum.

In the parable of the Good Samaritan, Jesus taught his surprised hearers that 'my neighbour is every man and woman'.[16] The point of the story is in the 'outsider' status of the person who was showing what a good neighbour is, the Samaritan. Jesus says to us: 'Do you likewise.' The call of Jesus does not contradict reason. Ultimately it is a call that summons us imaginatively to ground beyond reason.

Jesus' story of the Good Samaritan prompts the following question: how do we practise neighbourliness with each other within the household of the faith? In a social context, where it seems inevitable that there will be important personal differences of view and of perspective on moral and other questions, we owe it to one another to find ways of expressing friendship and respect even when there is disagreement.

St Augustine saw in the parable of the Samaritan an image of the human race. According to this interpretation, it was humanity that had been knocked down and robbed.[17] This image casts Jesus in the role of the Samaritan who comes to the rescue. These perspectives alter again the way in which we are accustomed to seeing things. They point up a certain richness of interpretation in the early church that was not afraid to seek out doctrinal messages even in the parables. In our own day, the original message rings out clearly. We can be reminded again that we owe to each other the gift of being a good neighbour, no matter who the per-

---

16. See Lk 10:29-37.
17. Augustine (354-430) Sermon 171. 3-5; See Origen (c. 185-254) Hom. 6, 4, see *The Divine Office*, 111, week 10, Thursday; and St Irenaeus (c. 130-200), *Against the Heresies*, Bk 3, 17, 1-3, see *The Divine Office*, Pentecost Sunday. Each has variations on this theme.

son is that we encounter. We owe each other a duty of support, trust, listening and care.

In another parable Jesus speaks to us of a father and his two very different sons.[18] At the centre of this story was the father who never gave up hoping for the eventual return of an erring son. We hear also of the outraged elder son, who refused to welcome his brother home. If we listen well to the parable, we realise that we can identify, each of us, with both the younger son and the elder brother as well. With the prodigal we can say: 'Father, I have sinned before heaven and before thee.' As we approach the eucharistic table to receive the Lord, we do so with those dispositions shown by the prodigal to his father. But with the elder son, we may find ourselves inclined to refuse to join in the father's banquet to honour the younger brother.

The Goodness of God

The 'goodness' of God poses a special challenge to the imagination. Initial impressions of goodness are laid down in childhood, and they tend to reflect things that a child values. The bonding that takes place between creatures can be a reminder of what takes place between believers and God. We would describe the instinct by which a mother protects her child, or a lioness her cub, as a good instinct. These initial human impressions of goodness lead us to reflect on what goodness in God might be.

Goodness belongs to God as a matter of course, a matter of definition. As part of the definition of God, in other words, it is a quality that exists in God because God exists. We are accustomed to thinking of goodness and evil as opposites because we can conclude, falsely, that if one were not there then the other would not be there either.[19] This is not quite true. God, we believe, is good, and in God there is no evil. The goodness of God, then, is a real property of being, of what is. While having no

18. Lk 15:11-32.
19. The 'evil' that we know of stems only from a reaction in that which has been created. St Thomas Aquinas famously defines evil as a 'lack' of goodness that ought to be present. Op. cit., 1a, 5, 48, 3. See F. C. Copleston, *Aquinas*, London 1955, pp 143ff.

direct knowledge of God's goodness, we can nonetheless shade in some aspects of God's nature as we understand it from the words of Jesus in order to bring this out.

While the transcendent or distant aspect of God is acknowledged in the gospels, it is never this transcendent aspect that is stressed. God appears embedded in the everyday world of the happiness, suffering, reward and pain of the people. God appears in the life of the poor man and the poor woman particularly, as one who is already present and already active among the neglected and the despised of the earth. There is an irony in this from our point of view, in that goodness at the divine level has much more of the human about it than we might ordinarily imagine. The goodness of God is much more practical and down to earth than we might have at first supposed. In the words of Jesus, God is portrayed as a loving and concerned father, always bending down to the level of his wayward and scattered children, always seeking to draw them to himself and to protect them from evil.

Jesus' descriptions of God are very like the descriptions of men and women that he gave in his own sermons.[20] These include 'the poor in spirit', 'those who mourn', 'the meek', 'those who hunger and thirst for righteousness', 'the merciful', 'the pure in heart', 'the peacemakers', 'those who are persecuted for righteousness' sake' and 'when men revile you and persecute you and utter all kinds of evil against you falsely on my account'. Each of these descriptions refers us to God as well as to his human creatures. Jesus, and by implication God, appears here not so much as some remote being, wrapped in pristine glory, but as one who is somehow more human than humans themselves.

The goodness of God, for the disciple of Jesus, turns not on abstract considerations of the perfect, but on very real and actual perceptions of the divine 'presence' that is with and within the human condition. That presence is always there, even in the worst of times. It is a presence of warmth and care, even when it

---

20. See Mt 3:5-11 & par.

is hidden from view and from feeling. The goodness of God is 'known' somehow, it manifests itself to the Christian conscience in the act of faith. And it is this goodness of God that causes us to be good.

The follower of Jesus recognises the voice of Jesus, the call of Jesus, within his or her own heart. It is always an invitation to be good or to protect the one who is weak from danger or from evil. And this is the voice that is always there because that is how Jesus is. He is one who encourages and forgives. He does not criticise or pull down; he does not 'break a bruised reed'.[21]

There is an immediate connection then from the goodness of God to the goodness that is in men and women. That is because goodness comes from God. We are good because God is good, and it is the goodness of God that flows over into us. Becoming good on our part is like coming from darkness to light. It is a movement from nothingness to being, from chaos to order, from rage to peace, from despair to hope. It is a movement towards the divine being. Peter said to Jesus on the occasion of the miraculous draught of fishes: 'depart from me, for I am a sinful man, O Lord.'[22] This conveys how it can feel to realise that one is in close proximity to the goodness of God. What is good in us is good because goodness itself is standing beside us, and yet somehow part of ourselves wants to hold back from it.

A key to a further understanding of this goodness is the practical and demanding concept of forgiveness, or a willingness to forgive. 'Forgiveness' is a key word in the vocabulary of goodness. Ours is a religion that forgives, and one that preaches forgiveness. It insists on forgiveness in season and out of season. For the disciple of Jesus, forgiveness is centred on the fact of the cross. When you look at the cross, and look beyond the religious image with which the world is now so familiar, and imagine something of the horror of the crucifixion of Jesus, or the horror of any crucifixion that ever has taken place, forgiveness is not a word that comes immediately to mind. The word 'anger' is

21. Is 42:1-4 (& Mt 12:18-21).
22. Lk 5-8.

much more likely to suggest itself. Yet for the follower of Jesus, the cross and forgiveness are inseparable; these two words 'cross' and 'forgiveness' are interchangeable. This is because we realise that our salvation turns upon the goodness and the forgiveness that were shown on the cross. We are saved by being forgiven in the context of Christ's death. Jesus' words of forgiveness spoken from the cross highlight this message for us.[23]

Forgiving others and asking for forgiveness are essential qualities of the self-consciousness of the ordinary Christian. They are essential to the message of Jesus. A quick run through the incidents in the gospels where forgiveness is mentioned would have to include at least the following: 'Forgive us our trespasses, as we forgive those who trespass against us';[24] 'I do not say to you seven times, but seventy times seven' (said to Peter on frequent forgiveness);[25] the parable of the unforgiving servant who misses the whole point of being forgiven himself;[26] and the parable of the Pharisee and the publican, where the publican alone calls himself a sinner and asks to be forgiven.[27] Because God who is good already forgives us, it is a kind of hypocrisy on our part if we do not in turn forgive others who offend us. As Jesus understood it, we have to become like God to the extent that we become forgiving followers of his. In this sense, we consciously take on the mantle of God's goodness, sinners that we are.

The Human Condition

Whatever way we approach it from, the reality of our condition seems to be one of having fallen from grace somehow. When we look at ourselves dispassionately, when we look at the world for which we are responsible, when we look into the meanness and selfishness that lurks in the heart of every one of us, we have to admit that we are far from good. What this throws into relief is

---

23. Lk 23:34.
24. Mt 6:12 & par.
25. Mt 18:22.
26. Mt 18:23-25.
27. Lk 18:9-14.

the fact that the human race is not only a race of rational creatures, but it is also a race of sinners. I am using each of these
words deliberately and carefully. Without God we are lost; in
some sense we have 'missed the mark' as the Greek word for sin
has it. This recognition has to belong to any moral awareness at
the very outset.

This awareness of the having fallen somehow in a moral
catastrophe that reaches back to our very origins is one that we
believe has been revealed by God. The stark figure of the cross
underlies it. The doctrine that sees the human race as first condemned and then redeemed probably constitutes the greatest
difficulty to many minds that are otherwise disposed to the
recognition of a Creator in our world today. It could be part of
the explanation why so many are giving up on religion while
embracing non-religious spiritualities that are not associated
with belief of this kind.

The moral insight of Christianity, however, is one that begins
with the sheer goodness of God. In each person, this insight
traces a movement away from sin and towards the goodness of
God. Every person is invited to situate himself in this dynamic
movement. Somehow the call of God and the recognition of our
own unworthiness are inextricably linked to one another. They
are part of the same perception. And so the implication of these
words can weigh heavily: 'Forgive us our trespasses as we forgive those who trespass against us.'

It is as ordinary persons, fragile and fallible, that we belong
to the Christian mystery. Christians make no claim on their own
behalf. Their strength and their faithfulness comes from God.
Their weakness is their own. To be aware of what being a moral
person demands does not in any way imply that one is better
than, or superior to, anybody else. It does not imply that one
finds it easier to forgive or that one finds it easier to give away
one's possessions. A person can know what is right, even as he
or she does what is wrong.

The awakening of the Christian faith in each person is a kin-
dling of forgiveness. It could even be the forgiveness of oneself.
There is no permanent place for bitterness in the soul, although

it is understandable that the soul can sometimes be bitter. By submerging each one of us in the waters of baptism, the Christian community calls upon God to banish all traces of sinfulness from us. From the moment of our baptism, we have to work to strengthen in ourselves the gift that we have been given. The church also acknowledges for us, in our name and with our consent, whether given personally or supplied for us by godparents, that we are sinners by birth and that we have been born into a race that is fallen.

While we are sinners by birth, we are not sinners by nature. As with the illnesses and deformities that may afflict us, sin does not belong to us by virtue of human nature. It is a circumstance of that nature, a circumstance that might not have occurred. We are heirs to that circumstance, as well as to human nature.

All of this follows from the realisation that the gift of faith comes from the goodness of God. In this realisation we accept the life and death of Jesus: he who is of God's own nature has been given to us and for us. It is an extraordinary human and divine transaction.

'The Narrow Gate'
Any form of pastoral care begins with a sense of one's own need for God. This includes an awareness of how sinful and unworthy we are before God and before others. We were created for better. In addition to our weakness and vulnerability, we need to attend to what might be called our 'best self'.

The best self is one that sets out to do God's will in everything. St Cyprian of Carthage gives this description of what God's will means:

'It means humility in conduct, steadfastness in faith, modesty in speech, justice in actions, mercy in deeds, discipline in morals; it is to be incapable of doing wrong to anyone and to bear patiently wrong done to us, to keep peace with the brethren, to love God with ones whole heart, to love him because he is the Father, to fear him because he is God.'[28]

28. Cyprian (210- 258), *On the Lord's prayer*, N. 15; see *The Divine Office*, III, week 11 of year, Wednesday.

Our 'best self' is balanced by knowledge of our 'worst self'. It is not difficult to imagine, from Cyprian's list, what the worst self implies. We know that the qualities he mentions do not come to us without a struggle. Particularly through the practice of prayer, we ask God to make it possible for us to be the kind of people we have been created to be.

Our best self is lived out not only at home, but also in the community. The Christian community should be permeated by a willingness to forgive. It is not simply a question of the private reconciliation of the individual sinner with God. The community itself, as well as its pastor, should be capable of at least wanting to make reconciliation with anybody who is alienated from it. The risen Christ makes this demand on us. We must be prepared to extend the hand of friendship in forgiveness and reconciliation. It is not possible to read and to accept the gospels and yet to remain closed to each other at these levels.

The community of the followers of Christ is a healing community. One reason for this is because each person in that community knows himself or herself to be a sinner. To be a Christian is to offer a helping hand, to be someone who understands, to be someone who is willing to walk the extra mile, as Jesus put it.[29]

It is the duty of the pastor or shepherd of souls to foster community awareness among God's people. Pastoral care, the work of the pastors of the church, seeks to create conditions that make Christian practice possible for the individual and for the community. We hear of the injunction to 'proclaim the message and, welcome or unwelcome, insist on it.'[30] Preaching, as well as encouraging people, often shows us ways of living that 'lean against' our more selfish tendencies.

There is always a natural curiosity about what will happen to others. We find it even on the lips of those who accompanied the Saviour.[31] Jesus teaches that in matters of virtue we should look

---

29. Mt 5:41.
30. 2 Tim 4:2.
31. See Lk 13:23 & par.

to ourselves first. He warns us many times that those who are now presumed to be in the right will be cast out, while many 'will come from east and west, and from north and south, and sit at table in the kingdom of God. And behold, some are last who will be first, and some are first who will be last.'[32]

In psalm 118 we read the prayer:

Open to me the gates of righteousness,
that I may enter through them
and give thanks to the Lord.

This is the gate of the Lord;
the righteous shall enter through it.[33]

Jesus also used the metaphor of a gate. In the passage known as the Sermon on the Mount, he said: 'Enter by the narrow gate, for the gate is wide and the way is easy that leads to destruction, and those who enter by it are many. For the gate is narrow and the way is hard, that leads to life, and those who find it are few.'[34] As St Luke tells it, Jesus was asked: 'Lord, will those that are to be saved be few?' On this occasion, we are told, he replied: 'Strive to enter by the narrow door, for many, I tell you, will seek to enter and will not be able.'[35] And in St John we read: 'I am the door; if any one enters by me, he will be saved, and will go in and out and find pasture.'[36] The 'narrow gate' is a metaphor of the way to God. By comparison with other gates, the gate that leads to God is a narrow one.

Jesus speaks also of the difficulty of threading a camel through the eye of a needle as an illustration of how difficult it will be for a rich man to enter the kingdom of heaven. Referring to the eye of a needle he said 'With men this is impossible, but with God all things are possible.'[37] The thrust and direction of the teaching of Jesus is clear to us; we know what we ourselves

---

32. Lk 13:30 & par.
33. Ps 118:19, 20.
34. Mt 7:13, 14.
35. Lk 13:23, 24.
36. Jn 10:9.
37. Mt 19:23-27.

must be and do. Nor should we make judgements about the
motives of other people who seem to be different from us.

Models of Gospel Living
The revelation of God is intended to be a message that is con-
veyed to the whole world, to people at all levels, to be understood by them and to be acted upon by them. The human race
may be visualised as a vast procession of people who are unknown and unremarkable. It is the human race as a whole that
has to be a reference point for any complete study of the meaning of faith and holiness.

If we study closely the message of revelation, we see that it
has constantly been refined from crude beginnings. It is not a
question of God revealing himself first in one way and later in a
different way. It is more a function of the human perception of
God. God's way to convince humanity was to first find ways of
identifying with it and with some of its primitive loyalties. This
also is what might have been expected: from the tribal partisan
God evident in parts of the early Old Testament, the God of battles, ever on 'our side', to the God who appeared to forsake his
own, and seemingly abandoned his people, yet never quite.
Then it is the God of all who seek him with a sincere heart, the
God of mercy and of justice, wonderful in his tenderness, fear-
some in his judgements. There is a rough and earthy texture to
things; some elements become much clearer in the more refined
later period and other elements mentioned in the former period
simply fall away.

Imaginatively, it can be difficult to picture the eternal destiny
of the human race as a whole. There are so many billions of people who have died and who can guess at how many billions remain to be born? We need some convincing image of the unity in
creation in order to come to terms with this difficulty. Motes in a
sunbeam suggests a picture of that which is tiny and insignificant being drawn into some kind of light. It might be helpful to
consider that the whole history of humanity has been played out,
so far, on one small planet that is infinitesimal in terms of the

universe as a whole. Or it might be helpful to put oneself into the much larger frame that brings together the creation and its creator.

We should remember also that each human being is a separate and distinct individual. Hence there can be no one model of holiness, although we are each called to imitate Jesus, but in our own circumstances and in our own way. There is always the temptation to think that the life of a saint is not for oneself.

So our models for gospel living will have to be many and varied, capable of reflecting the needs and realities of many cultures, different social classes, different occupations, both sexes, single and married, sick and well. Every person that is born, while receiving more or less the same human nature, receives a very different personal and social inheritance from that of his or her neighbour. God knows exactly who we are, we believe, and he has called us to himself in a manner that can maximise our goodness and our particular strengths.

Prayer: an invitation to speak with God
In this closing section, we will examine briefly the reality of prayer. It is probably true to say that most prayer belongs to situations where the existence of God is taken for granted, where the individual speaks unselfconsciously to someone who is known and trusted. But prayer belongs also to situations of doubt and great perplexity concerning God. People are often hard pressed by the circumstances of life and pushed by them to address some words to a creator, without even their knowing if such a being exists. Prayers of desperation we might call them, but prayers nonetheless.

The significance of prayer is not so much in the kneeling, or in the going to church, although these have their importance. Prayer is, basically, a trusting communication with God, one that takes place in the midst of everyday things. It encompasses the whole of human experience, both the blessings of life and the concerns and tribulations that we encounter. It eventually becomes a habitual communication that takes place despite the difficulties and the distractions that are occasioned by it.[38]

An invitation to speak with God can be found in the words of psalm 139:

O Lord, you search me and you know me,
You know my resting and my rising,
You discern my purpose from afar.
You mark when I walk or lie down,
All my ways lie open to you.

Before ever a word is on my tongue
you know it, O lord, through and through.
Behind and before you besiege me,
your hand ever laid upon me.
Too wonderful for me this knowledge,
too high, beyond my reach.

O where can I go from your spirit,
Or where can I flee from your face?
If I climb the heavens, you are there.
If I lie in the grave, you are there.

If I take the wings of the dawn
and dwell at the sea's furthest end,
even there your hand would lead me,
your right hand would hold me fast.

If I say: 'Let the darkness hide me
and the light around me be night,
even darkness is not dark for you
and the night is as clear as the day.'

These lines were written down some two thousand five hundred years ago, in Jerusalem. They were associated with the liturgy in the Temple. We hear in them a real sense of the com-

---

38. See Newman, *Parochial and Plain Sermons* I, op. cit., 11, p 145. There he discusses the 'difficulty of entering into the meaning of (our prayers), when we do attend to them'. What is needed is the confidence to go ahead, and humility in our necessarily imperfect way.

munication between the individual and God. It is a 'one to one' relationship. The focus is on a personal and exclusive interaction that takes place at the deepest levels of the person. It is a classic of prayer.[39] The remainder of the psalm goes on in this vein:

For it was you who created my being,
knit me together in my mother's womb.
I thank you for the wonder of my being,
for the wonders of all your creation.

Already you knew my soul,
my body held no secret from you
when I was being fashioned in secret
and moulded in the depths of the earth.

And so the psalm continues; there are twenty-one verses in all. Some of the final verses express hatred reserved for one's enemies. As has been observed, the words 'love your enemies' had not yet been spoken; they were still a long way off.

Psalm 139 can put a person who is open to meeting God immediately in touch with him. This is true of many of the psalms. People of many different religious beliefs and of none find comfort in them. They have been prayed in thousands of different situations since they were first written down.

To begin to pray is to insert oneself into a largely unseen community of need. It is a community that is engaged, more or less, in an outpouring of faith in what cannot be seen, an outpouring of hope in what often seems hopeless. The reality of a corresponding 'other world' where prayer is heard is attested to in the steady, confident assertion of many rational and reasonable people that God exists and loves us, even when the evidence of this love is not always apparent.

Prayer begins with the recognition that one is already known, rather than with the desire to know. Knowing God in

39. In Job 23:8-9, we see a reversal of the imagery that is used in psalm 139. Yet it is clear from the context that the same meaning is intended: 'If I go eastward, he is not there; or westward – still I cannot see him. If I seek him in the north, he is not to be found, invisible still when I turn to the south. And yet he knows of every step I take.'

prayer begins to grow with time and patience. The believer grows into it as he or she grows in knowledge of God and of the world that God has made. He or she grows in faith, in trust, in confidence and in a willingness to rely on one's own judgement, under God. All of these qualities come together in this most important of human acts, the act whereby God converses with us and we converse with God.

CHAPTER TEN

Holiness

Christians believe that the gradual narrative that moves from the Old Testament to the New is the unfolding of the work of the Holy Spirit as well as being the revelation of the Son of God. The narrative moves to the world of incarnation of God's Son at Bethlehem in Palestine. This 'becoming flesh'[1] is a high point of the development of the plan, or 'mystery' as it is called, of the involvement between God and creation. In this mystery, all is holy. Everything is holy because everything comes from God, who is the Holy One.

Over and against this perception of reality that is based on God stands all that is not God; that is, all that is outside of God, although God is the ultimate creator of all that is. The word profane refers to this aspect of not God in creation. Profane describes the limited, worldly sphere of human activity as opposed to the sacred. Most of us earn our daily bread in what is called the profane world. The holy and the profane interface with each other every day, and not necessarily in any kind of enmity.

In becoming a human person, God has crossed over the boundary between the holy and the profane. In a sense, God has become profane, which seems like a contradiction in terms. Or, everything has become holy, or has had the perspective of holiness opened up to it. Let us look at this a little further.

If we think of the idea of bonding, the special relationship that comes to exist between a mother and a child, we can form some analogous notion of what is happening when we refer to holiness. In a sense, everything remains the same before a bond-

---

1. See Jn 1:14.

ing takes place between the mother and baby. Yet, it makes no sense at all to say that, because the bonding is not visible, it is not there; a special relationship has been established. This relationship is of the utmost importance for the individuals concerned even though it is invisible. For the person who believes, a bonding of some kind has opened up between him or her and the Creator. The name of this analogous bonding between the individual and the Creator is holiness. It is through that bonding, when it has taken place, that everything else in the world is viewed by the religious believer, whether that person is in pain or at peace.

Holiness and Grace

The word holy defines God in some manner. In God, it refers to apartness, distinctness from creation. In this primary meaning it refers to the divinity alone. In a sense, we hardly know the meaning of the word holy other than to say that it describes God. When we say that God shares with us the holiness that belongs to God alone, we say that we are given a share in Godliness.

Divine goodness makes itself known to us when we reflect on the self- giving of God. We read:

His state was divine,
Yet he did not cling
To his equality with God
But emptied himself
To assume the condition of a slave
And became as men are ...[2]

God always comes to us as complete gift, given by God. It is never possible for the human spirit to get to God first. And so there is a natural flowing over of goodness and of being that

---

2. Phil 2:6ff. This text is thought to be an ancient hymn to Christ. It may have been slightly altered by the hand of Paul to bring out the more shameful aspects of Christ's abasement, particularly his death as a criminal on a cross. Jerome Murphy O'Connor, *Paul, a critical life*, Oxford, 1996, pp 225-226.

begins in the act of creation, and that begins again in the acts of inspiration and incarnation whereby God becomes man. All of this is grace.

Again, reflection on what happens when a mother and child bond with each other carries us forward a little. Just as the child gradually imbibes a certain trust and confidence in the world from its mother's nurture, the person imbibes a trust and confidence in the existence of God through grace: a trust and a confidence that are gifted to us by God. This confidence in the soul, even in the presence of difficulties and of great uncertainties, is the gift of grace. And so, in the context of God's existence, the believer can take hold of the whole mystery of his or her own existence. Existence is no longer a puzzle that cannot be further explored.

The grace of God enables us to accept the fact of the presence of God, whether it be a matter of God's existence 'in heaven' or of God's existence 'on earth'. 'The Word was made flesh' indicates something about total presence to and with the human family. God's being present to us on earth each day is more important and more fundamental than anything else.

Ideally speaking, God's presence to us disposes us to a readiness to do his will at all times. This readiness can begin to become second nature to us. Such readiness is completed in the act of obedience, a concept not well understood in our time. Obedience is not simply bowing to the will of God. Rather, it is an entering into that whole providence of God. It is a participation which will be different for each human being, because each one brings to it different gifts and unique circumstances. Yet it is an obedience that is always consistent with a person's intelligence and freedom, although it may be that elements of darkness and uncertainty accompany it. The supreme example of such obedience was that of Jesus in the Garden at Gethsemane, where he prayed in deep anguish:

'My Father,' he said, 'if it is possible, let this cup pass me by. Nevertheless, let it be as you, not I, would have it.'[3]

---

3. Mt 26:39.

A way of thinking about God's grace is to reflect on the 'epiphanies' that we encounter. An epiphany occurs whenever something hidden and unforeseen discloses itself. In the Christian calendar, the feast of the Epiphany takes place some twelve days after Christmas when a fuller disclosure of the birth of the messiah was made known. Epiphanies surprise us. It could be in something like the unfolding of a flower, when aspects of the nature of all development and beauty are momentarily disclosed to us. Or it could be in a person's suffering, when the very fragility of human life comes home to us.

Divine grace moves in epiphanies. In preparation for this book, one of my conversations hit upon epiphanies in ordinary life. Martin's acceptance of the providence of God in the incident he describes below is striking. His familiarity with the New Testament undoubtedly played a role in his experience:

I had an experience some years ago, which in my worst moments of unbelief stayed with me. You could say was it a hallucination. After coming through a very bad period of trial, I was sitting one day overlooking the sea, and suddenly I was conscious of a white figure standing beside me. Now it wasn't tangible ... and a voice, not that I heard it, but it was spiritual, said to me: 'I have prayed for thee that thy faith fail not, and do thou being once converted, confirm thy brethren.'[4] And that stayed with me for years, for at least ten years afterwards ... I had no faith, but that stayed with me as a bulwark against throwing anything aside. That actually happened, and I had to hang on to it: it wasn't my imagination, it was an actual event. Now talking about it is not good; I know that it is not good to talk about it. It is like telling the plot of a play. That is the danger ...

Martin's episode puts one in mind of the words that Jesus addressed to Peter on the seashore after the resurrection. Martin was overlooking the sea, and very conscious of his seeming lack of faith, as it would appear that Peter also was when Jesus appeared to him.

In the structure of Christian belief, epiphany leads on to

4. See Jn 21:15-17.

proclamation. Proclamation is part of the gift of belief. We cannot keep the gift to ourselves. It usually happens, of course, that this gift of proclamation must find many discreet ways of expressing itself because to be overtly religious is frequently to be seriously unwelcome in the profane world.

Sacrament: a context
A believing people, as we have seen, needs to belong to a community of some kind in which our worshipping of God is shared with each other. Yet the church is more than this. It is a community of saints, people called to holiness. We are invited to imagine the church as an actual body, like a human body with head and parts, which enters into the interior life of God in heaven.[5]

The discovery of the infinitesimal in our own bodies, the atom and the cell, helps the imagination here. Each of our bodies is made up of millions and millions of cells, each of which contributes to our overall health and wellbeing. Jesus Christ is the head of his spiritual body, that is, the community of believers; a body that is invited to share in the internal activity of God; almost 'as of right' we might say. He is linked with every believing soul, past and present. The Holy Spirit bonds us all, each to Jesus and to one another. It is as if we enter now into the life of God as a corporate entity, and Jesus is our head, while the Holy Spirit is our breathing.

A key term in Christian theology is the word mystery. It is a term that can easily be misunderstood outside of its proper context. In theology, mystery refers to that which is ultimately beyond the scope of our intelligence to fully understand. Outside of theology mystery tends to be used as an alternative designation for words like puzzle or conundrum, or in detective stories as a synonym for unsolved crime.

As we have seen, the paschal mystery refers to the passion, death and resurrection of Christ as an abiding event into which we are all drawn. In this respect it denotes a reality that will always exceed the human capacity to grasp it fully. However, we

---

5. 1 Cor 12:12-13ff.

believe that God has given us sacraments that enable us to engage with the mystery, even if not understanding it fully.

The sacraments of the church are mysteries in the theological sense. When, in the celebration of the eucharist, the priest says the words of Jesus: 'Do this in commemoration of me',[6] he refers to this sense of mystery. Jesus is present 'sacramentally' in our world today as we recall his last supper and all that it entailed. It is his death and his resurrection enacted in our own life context. He is present to us, and we to him.

We have already noted where the question was asked: 'How can this man give us his flesh to eat?' In the eucharist, we are dealing, obviously, with what cannot be completely understood. The people of Palestine then were no different from us now in their normal understanding of things. At the end of the passage, in answer to Jesus, Peter says: 'Lord, to whom shall we go? You have the words of eternal life; and we have believed, and have come to know that you are the Holy One of God.'[7] The depth of the eucharistic mystery cannot be fully comprehended. Yet Peter shows us the way forward with this profession of faith.

From this perspective, we can begin to appreciate more fully the meaning of the sacraments of the church. Baptism is a simple rite of initiation whereby we receive the gift of the Holy Spirit and are incorporated into the church. Confirmation can be a more elaborate rite in which the new Christian personally appropriates the grace of baptism at a more adult stage. Penance is a rite of forgiveness whereby we are restored to our baptismal grace when this has been lost by our own failure. Eucharist is the rite of thanksgiving whereby we remember what it was that Jesus did by dying on the cross, and in and through which we communicate with him, present in the human community, on earth and in heaven. Ordination is the rite whereby pastors and ministers are provided for the community. Anointing is the rite whereby someone in serious illness is consecrated to God and the community prays for the healing of that person. Marriage is

6. Lk 22:19.
7. Jn 6:52-70.

the rite whereby two people promise and give themselves to each other as husband and wife in the believing community.

All of the sacraments of the church are mystical acts in which the Christian community is grounded. They are simple acts, publicly performed, with a sincere intention, and with a minimum of 'material'. A bowl of water for baptism, some bread and wine for the eucharist. The words 'I do' express the consent of husband and wife. The sacraments mediate to us, in symbolic form, the graces of a world that is unseen by us. They validate and enable us to live the life of now with its challenges, its smiles and tears.

Above all else, the community of believers is a kind of vast sacrament, an effective sign of that bonding instinct that God's providence has brought into play for each of us. We do not come to God in isolation. Our loving of God and our loving of each other are deeply intertwined. As it is in the great commandment: 'that we should love God with all our mind … and love our neighbour as ourselves.'[8] Our love for God cannot be separated from our love for one another.

The implications of holiness
The gospel image of the yeast that lifts the loaf of bread suggests itself here.[9] We live in a world where there is knowledge as well as ignorance, where some are full while others starve, where some are being born as others die. In this human family, the invisible presence of Jesus is mediated by his word, his sacraments and by the example of his followers. This is the mysterious context of the body of Christ on earth. It is a context in which the believer holds that Jesus is present to every soul, or wishes to be.

An awareness of the outreach of God's call to every human person is part of the vocation to holiness. The holy person is one who is pre-disposed to see 'the face of God' in every human face. This inclusiveness of the Christian community's understanding of its role in the world should be evident from the gospels.

---

8. Mt 22:35-40.
9. Mt 13:33 & par.

Throughout the Old and the New Testaments, there is ample evidence to show that an aspect of the most basic understanding of God's people was that it be of service to the wider world. We find it in the promises to Abraham, we find it again in the psalms, and we find it in the basic thrust of the missionary work of the apostles.[10]

Inclusiveness should mean an attitude of openness and understanding to what people already sincerely believe about God. We cannot hope to influence people, or to be influenced, as we would wish, unless and until we have learned first to listen and to be present to them as they are. Our consciousness of epiphanies should prepare us for moments of disclosure that are occasions of grace in places we had not expected them. It ought not to be any great surprise to us to find that the holiness we prize is already possessed by the men and women of faiths other than our own. Do we not find in the gospels how Jesus marvels at the faith he found in some of the pagans?[11] Do we not find in the Acts of the Apostles how Peter marvelled at the faith he found in the centurion Cornelius?[12] Too often in the past, the history of theology has been impoverished by a false culture of exclusiveness towards other denominations and other faiths. The way forward to a greater understanding of each other for all people can only be through a greater respect on the part of all for the sincerely held traditions of each.

An important implication of holiness is the fact that, already here on earth, we have begun a journey that we dare to hope will terminate in God. Some sense of the ultimate destination is present in every journey. How do we anticipate what life in heaven with God will be like? In some respects we have no idea of life in heaven. In other respects, however, we can infer something about heaven from what we already know about this life. Eternity with God will be shared with the humble of the earth; it will be an eternity of wonder and praise; it will be an eternity of

---

10. See Jn 20:21; Acts 22:21 & par.
11. Mt 15:28 & par.
12. Acts 10:34.

reciprocal love, giving and receiving. This much our Christian faith confirms.

All of this is brought together in the Sermon on the Mount,[13] also called the Beatitudes, and in the special prayer that Jesus gave us, Our Father.[14] The prayer of Jesus begins by recognising the place of God who is Our Father in heaven in our own consciousness. If one accepts the existence and presence of a universal creator, a Father, then it is but a short step to accept this person as Our Father. Jesus shows us this step.[15] If God is our father, then anybody can call God father. And if anybody can call God father, then that must mean that everybody is either my brother or my sister. It is an implication that is simple and straightforward. This is not so much something that one has to be taught to believe; rather it is something that follows naturally upon the fact of belief. It is here that the church's social teaching takes root. And it is here that the Christian vision of other religions must be based.

The prayer continues, 'hallowed be thy name'. All of our first impulses in prayer are ones that turn to God in the act of praise. 'Thy kingdom come, thy will be done', the prayer continues, 'on earth as it is in heaven'. Our consciousness of the world is shaped in such a way that it includes the consciousness of heaven. Just as heaven is, so must earth seek to become.

With the words: 'give us this day our daily bread', we ask that what we have received will be sustained for today. 'Forgive us our trespasses, as we forgive those who trespass against us' encourages us to have the same attitude to those who ask forgiveness from us, as God has towards us who ask forgiveness from him. The prayer finishes with the words 'lead us not into temptation and deliver us from evil', a reflection on our vulnerability throughout life. In some ancient versions that have been influenced by liturgy it concludes: 'for yours is the kingdom, the power and the glory, now and forever. Amen', which brings the

---

13. Mt 5:2-12 & par.
14. See note 12 above.
15. See the prayer 'Our Father ...' Mt 6:9-13 & par.

mind back to its focus on what lies ahead, the eternal goal for which we have all been created and redeemed.

The New Testament speaks in several places of eternal loss and of the punishment of the wicked. There is a danger that we can so easily project this fate on to other people. We should not project the idea of God as judge onto others in a way that excludes ourselves. Not to countenance the possibility of our own failure with God is to fall into the sin of presumption. Such presumption is a very negative response, or an indifferent response, to the love offered by God. God is redeemer and he is judge. The believer approaches him with reverence and with confidence. Fears that are rightly engendered by the possibility of eternal loss should not be allowed to overcome the basic optimism and hope that are engendered by God's love of each person.

Attitudes of heart

If we look back at the Christian writings that were current in the early first and second centuries AD, we get a sense of the determination of Christians to change themselves as well as to change the world around them. This determination of personal renewal is sometimes referred to as the 'ascetic' tradition, from the Greek word *askesis* meaning an athletic exercise or discipline. The ascetic Christians of the early church had no illusions about the need for personal conversion of heart and soul that the following of the gospel required. They wanted to put themselves right with regard to God first and, then, with regard to their fellow men and women. They believed that they would have to work hard on themselves so as to bring themselves into line and to practise the style of life indicated in the gospels. For the Christian, an ascetic practice of fasting or of almsgiving and, not infrequently, both, arises in an attitude of heart that identifies with the mission and the suffering of Jesus.

'The Didache' (Teaching of the Twelve Apostles), which has some of its roots in the Old Testament,[16] shows that the ascetic

---

16. Deut 11:26-28.

life was part and parcel of the daily life of the church from earliest times. Going without food deliberately helped to focus the mind and to fix it on God. This regime was very similar to that practised by devout Jews everywhere, and Jews brought it with them into Christianity. In another second century work, 'The Shepherd' of Hermas, the injunction to fast is linked specifically to the care of widows and orphans and those in need. In a very practical way, the person is told to consume only bread and water for the day of the fast, and to put the money thereby saved to one side and give it to the poor.[17]

We have here a call to give up something that is one's own in order to remind oneself about God and about one's neighbour. The gesture of sacrifice embraces also those in need, those who may be outside of one's normal or domestic circle of care. It is a two-fold consciousness and a two-fold invitation. God and 'the poor man or woman at the gate' are linked in thought. This is the association of ideas that speaks to us. Christians and Jews everywhere recognise in it a call from beyond as well as a call from within. This call does not always find a ready or willing response in us. Yet it is the hearing of this call that gives us a true sense of who we are and of who our neighbours are.

The fourth century preacher John Chrysostom expressed this call thus with a characteristic depth and irony:

Would you honour the body of Christ? Do not despise his nakedness; do not honour him here in church clothed in silk vestments and then pass him by unclothed and frozen outside. Remember that he who said, 'This is my body', and made good his words, also said, 'You saw me hungry and gave me no food', and, 'In so far as you did it not to one of these, you did it not to me.' In the first sense the body of Christ does not need clothing but worship from a pure heart. In the second sense it does need clothing and all the care that we can give it ... What is the use of loading Christ's table with gold cups while he himself is starving? Feed the hungry and then if you

17. Hermas, sim. V. iii. Lake, *The Apostolic Fathers*, Vol 2.

have any money left over, spend it on the altar table. Will you make
a cup of gold and withhold a cup of water?[18]

Every day on television, we are confronted with images of famine and want. During the seasons of Advent and Lent, in particular, the church invites each of us to put on the mantle of the penitent and to respond personally to this call from those who are in need. This is the teaching of Jesus that is confirmed by our own intelligence, as if it were spoken today for the first time. It is one side of a remarkable coin. On the reverse side of this coin is the image of the merciful God who welcomes each one who turns to him.

The appeal of St John Chrysostom catches us also in another way. We are reminded by it that we are all in debt to Christ and to a greater or a lesser extent to one another. The comfort that I enjoy contrasts with the poverty that he knew and with the poverty of many of my fellow human beings, whether close to home or farther off. It is a comfort that comprises of so much: education, opportunity, good name, good fortune, money, as well as of family and friends. It is a comfort that, for the most part, certainly, I have not earned. Yet for others, through no fault of theirs, life has been an experience of poverty and of sorrow. In a world in which we are brothers and sisters to every man and woman, it is not unnatural that our hearts should be drawn to some responsibility for them, and to care for those who have been less fortunate than we have, for whatever reason.

Holiness requires a view of history, particularly in respect of the relief of oppression and, in modern times, of the importance of education and the emancipation of those who live in poverty. Genuine belief in God is accompanied by an awareness of our co-responsibility for history. These elements go together in a trusting and a self-giving manner.

---

18. St John Chrysostom (349-407) Hom. 50. 3-4; quoted in *The Divine Office* III, week 21, Saturday. We find irony also in the words of Caesarius of Arles (470-542) on this same theme: Sermon 25, 1; see *The Divine Office*, III, week 17, Monday.

In the distant times of the Old Testament, we find a concern for the widow and the orphan, and for 'the poor' as a whole class.[19] There they are represented as the people who, despite their misfortune, are close to God. We find this message again in the New Testament that is exemplified in the teaching of Jesus in the beatitudes. We find that same message in the agreement made later in Jerusalem between the apostles when they agreed on Paul and Barnabas's mission to the pagans.[20] The final exhortation they received was that they should help the poor.

In Christian symbolism, it is the 'heart' that is often seen as the seat of the personality. In this way of thinking, God too has a heart, and it is the heart of God that reaches out to the human family. We have an example of this heart metaphor or heart speech when Jesus says that there is more joy in heaven when one sinner repents, more joy than there is for ninety-nine who have no need of repentance.[21] It is a form of speech that can be understood only from within a feeling or a sympathy that prioritises human reconciliation with God and with each other above all else.

A person may be grieving for a loved one in pain, or seriously ill, or suffering some other great need. That person may not be able to directly assuage the pain of the other, nor do anything to diminish it. Yet, he or she shares in the suffering of the other, differently but, perhaps, not less in fact. This example, moreover, illustrates something of the transcendent nature of human grief and of divine grief. These realities are very much part of the world in which we live.

Mary, the mother of Jesus
At the heart of the Christian message is a lowly village culture. The village of Nazareth, where Mary lived, belonged to such a setting. It is a quiet culture with unremarkable sounds. The words that describe it are variously translated as lowly, humble

---

19. Ex 22:21; 23:1-9; Is 1:17; Ps 67:5-6; Ps 146:7-9b.
20. Gal 2:10.
21. Lk 15:7.

and poor. They convey something of the ordinariness and silence of a place like Nazareth. Nazareth is not mentioned anywhere in the Old Testament. The apostle Nathaniel asks, 'Can anything good come out of Nazareth?'[22] The Hebrew word that might be used for its inhabitants refers to 'the humble people of God', the *anawim*, people who are like slaves in the main, people who are refugees. These words are central to an understanding of the place and of the people. They portray people who are humble, not unlike many of those in Europe and elsewhere who were hounded into death camps in the twentieth century. The person at the centre of Nazareth, from the point of view of God, is Mary. The great model of holiness is Mary, the mother of Jesus.

At the centre of Mary's call to holiness is the fact that she was invited by God to become the mother of Jesus. God invited her to all that she became. Mary gave herself to bring the incarnation of God into being. What we know through the exchanges that took place is that she understood something of this and that she said 'yes' to it.[23] Everything else about Mary follows from these facts of her invitation and her response. From St Luke we know that she was a reflective person: he wrote of her 'and his mother kept all these things in her heart'.[24]

It is too easy, perhaps, to run together all the events of the life and death and resurrection of Christ, the coming of the Holy Spirit and the founding of the church, and to situate Mary in some way that presumes that she always knew and understood the way that things were unfolding. We do not know what Mary understood of her son in those years, other than that she followed him and that she believed in him. We do not know what was going through Mary's mind as Jesus was crucified. She saw him die and, according to a familiar image, she helped to take down the body and bury it. Arguably we are dealing here with a faith that was as raw as any, with a 'hope against hope' that she was not mistaken in her belief. Might not she have thought, in all

22. Jn 1:46.
23. Lk 1:38.
24. Lk 2:51.

reasonableness, as Martha did of Jesus on the death of her brother Lazarus, 'If you had been here, my brother would not have died …'[25]

Mary knew that the child she bore was some mystery that was beyond her, but that knowledge was sufficient to sustain her hope throughout the awful events she was to witness and during the long years of persecution and martyrdom that characterised the early life and dispersal of the church. Mary is a person who symbolises all human beings who are waiting for God. She waits and she believes, she hopes against hope. In what ways was she tempted in later years to re-interpret what happened to her then? We do not know.

Tradition has it that Mary was assumed into heaven. It was a kind of death, and yet it was different, we are led to believe, from other instances of death. A very widespread and ancient tradition speaks of the 'dormition' of Mary.[26] Dormition comes from the Latin word for sleep. Christian faith asserts that she is already bodily in heaven where all of us hope one day to be, body and soul. In other words, the completeness that Christians yearn for and look forward to after death has already been granted to Mary.

As a symbol for all the waiting people of God, Mary is a model of faith. She shows us that silent and effective state of mind whereby we each take hold of God and God takes hold of us. Women and men may appropriate such a quality of mind in any walk of life. Thinking of Mary, we might raise our minds to God and make the prayer: 'Lord, make me to be one of your chosen people …' There is no reason why we may not take the

---

25. Jn 11:21.
26. *New Catholic Encyclopaedia*, op. cit., Vol 1, Assumption of Mary (J. W. Langlinais) 797-801; Vol 4, Dormition of the Virgin (D. F. Hickey) 875-6; Vol 9 (J. Lafontaine-Dosogue) Mary, Blessed Virgin, Iconography of, 271-281. The story or legend of the *'Transitus Mariae'*, dates from the fifth century, when Mary was proclaimed 'Mother of God'. It is found in many ancient Eastern languages, and in the West there are, apart from the Latin texts, Irish versions of the childhood and death of Mary.

prayer given by St Luke from the days when she was expecting her child, and make it our own.

My soul magnifies the Lord,
and my spirit rejoices in God my Saviour,
for he has regarded the low estate of his handmaiden.
For behold, henceforth all generations will call me blessed;
for he who is mighty has done great things for me,
and holy is his name.
And his mercy is on those who fear him
from generation to generation.
He has shown strength with his arm,
he has scattered the proud in the imagination of their hearts,
he has put down the mighty from their thrones,
and exalted those of low degree;
he has filled the hungry with good things,
and the rich he has sent empty away.
He has helped his servant Israel,
in remembrance of his mercy,
as he spoke to our fathers,
to Abraham and to his posterity forever.[27]

We have here a total giving of self to God, not so much for what one is, but because one has been chosen. Being chosen makes it possible to be whatever it is that God seems to want. Christian belief is based on the premise that each of us has been chosen by God.

If we let our gaze wander among the verses of Mary's prayer, we recognise again features that are already familiar from the preaching of Jesus, or from his prayer. These features did not spring unannounced upon an unsuspecting world. A quiet and reflective reading of much of the Old Testament shows that they have been gradually emerging into consciousness over centuries. In the New Testament, we have a more completed picture. Faith is not seeing God but believing in him. If we find that we can begin to see the world as God sees it, then it is not so far from this belief that Christian holiness begins.

27. Lk 1:46-55.

CHAPTER ELEVEN

The Believing Community

A willingness to see things from a religious perspective, from the perspective that includes God, is something that we each make possible for one another. Knowledge of God is something that each person discovers, as we have seen, primarily from somebody else. It is a willingness that comes mainly from human contact, not from any institutional, or academic, or remote contact. Any human person can be a contact point for any other. The good example of each person shows forth the message of God. It is in the ordinary example of real people that God speaks to us first.

This emphasis on ordinary people with regard to the knowledge of God in our lives is not intended to denigrate the church. The church, whether viewed as community of believers or as institution, represents a necessary element, even if it manifests itself in an imperfect manner. That element is the stable and ongoing guarantee of the divine presence in the wider world. It is a focus for the unity of all sincere religious belief. It is an aspect of God's mark on history. But it is an element that is to be distinguished from, but not necessarily separated from, that primary experience of perceiving God that belongs to our moment of first contact with him. That first contact is one that usually comes through another living person.

Since earliest times, Christians have made the mistake of imagining the church to be a kind of state, with a ruler and with subjects. Many people, misguidedly in my opinion, give over their lives to defending such an institution at all costs. It seems to me that the truth of the matter is simpler than this. Spiritually, what is at work in the world is the heart of God. When we come together to speak of and to celebrate this awareness, we are the church.

Structures are frequently very imperfect and in need of change for the better, including the structures of the church. The primary task of faith is to know and love God in return for his love of us. And knowing God also means sharing that knowledge and love, however imperfectly, with somebody else.

There can be a tendency to think of the individual as solitary before God, which, indeed, in a sense, each person is. But it is a temptation to imagine oneself solely as alone with God without the benefit or hindrance of other people. Seen from the perspective of the Christian community, such a view is a false one. While we are believers, we are also and always members of a community of belief.

The interaction between the individual and the community to which he or she belongs is a commonplace of social thinking. In ordinary life, we depend on the community not only for our genetic inheritance, for conception, birth and nurture, but also for the language that we speak and the culture and the sub-cultures with which we identify. It is no different from this in the matter of belief. We draw the structures and the stories that go to make up our own identity from the wider community of which each of us is a part.

If we look at the scriptures, we can see clearly the principle of community that is at work there. In the Old Testament, the Word of God came to be known and believed through the ordinary lives of the people of Israel over a period of more than fifteen hundred years. It need not be supposed that Israel was considered a 'worthy' nation, deserving of this gift. In fact, throughout the scriptures, what strikes us again and again is the unfaithfulness and wilfulness of the people, their capacity to turn their backs on what God has revealed of himself and to return to former idolatrous ways, and their own awareness of this situation. The prophets frequently pointed to the fact that what made Israel great was not any inherent virtue on its own part because it was a small and insignificant people on the world stage.

According to them, Israel's greatness lay solely in the fact that it had been chosen by God to be the bearer of his word.[1] It was Israel's 'chosen-ness' that marked it out in the eyes of God, nothing else.

In the New Testament, we find the traces of the believing community in every text. It was this community that gave shape to the documents that we now possess, whether gospels or epistles or other writings, like the Acts of the Apostles or the Book of Revelation. And it need not be supposed that this community of believers from which the New Testament was to emerge was a community without fault, misunderstandings and backsliding. One has only to look at the letters to the seven churches that are found in the Book of Revelation to see how deeply compromised some of these early communities could be.[2] In other words, from the beginning we might say, the different members of the first faith communities lived side by side with each other in an atmosphere that included misunderstanding, betrayal, apostasy, and clinging to belief against all the odds, as well as fellowship and mutuality. Even as they recalled his passion and the last supper, the first Christians recalled the betrayal of Jesus by many of his own.

We are neither any better nor any worse than those who have gone before us, although we may be tempted, on occasion, either to idealise them or to look down on them. We admire their holiness when it is recalled, as in the lives of the saints; and we recoil from their barbarity, as when they burned heretics. We are, even as the first Christians were, ordinary believers who inherit our unique spaces in time and in human culture. We are people with the same virtues and advantages, more or less, as they had, and with vices and drawbacks similar to theirs, although such vices may be expressed differently in our time. To be a community of ordinary believers is to have the honesty and openness to identify with human ordinariness and to trust as fully as we can in God's unconditional love for us all.

1. See Deut 8:1-20 & par.
2. Rev 2:1- 3. 22.

A believing community is a community in which the experience of faith is shared with others and transmitted from one generation of believers to the next. And the community is one that is constantly open to the drawing in of new members from outside of itself. It will become evident, I hope, that a believing community is central to the meaning of faith.

The Descent of the Spirit

Our reflection begins with the third person of the Blessed Trinity, the Holy Spirit. Until that manifestation of God, the focus had been on the man Jesus. Some time after Jesus had ascended into heaven, his followers were gathered with his mother Mary in an upper room of a house. They were frightened about what might happen to them 'for fear of the Jews'. We read that then the Holy Spirit descended upon them in fire and tongues, and this spirit inhabited them in a manner which was to change them utterly for the remainder of their days.[3]

Properly speaking, despite all that had gone on before with the teaching and the passion and death and even the resurrection of Jesus, it was this event in the upper room that marked the beginning of the believing community. Up to this point the apostles and the disciples had indeed been instructed and guided by the Risen Jesus, and their confidence in him had to a certain extent been restored. They knew something of what he expected them to do and to be. With this event, however, the Holy Spirit, that is the spirit that was sent and put into them by Jesus, in a sense the very spirit of Jesus himself, took them over from within. That spirit made each of them into a new Jesus on earth, living and acting and preaching in his name to all the nations.

In the gospels we read that the Holy Spirit had already overshadowed Mary at the time of the annunciation, and that the Spirit had descended upon Jesus at his baptism in the Jordan. The disciples still, however, understood imperfectly the teaching about God and the Spirit that they would come to know and preach. In the documents that emerged from the communities

---

3. Acts 2:1-13.

that were founded from this original group, we can see how their knowledge of God as Father, Son and Holy Spirit gradually clarified and, indeed, reached its final form in which we now know it only several centuries later.

It was only with their separation from the physical Jesus that their possession of this fullness of knowledge became possible for them.[4] After the ascension of Jesus to the Father, the primary carrier of the word of God was the Holy Spirit to the early community and its successors. This word of God, although communicated in various ways by Jesus during his lifetime, only comes together finally after he has departed this life. The authors of the New Testament differ from each other somewhat in their recounting of the descent of the Holy Spirit on them, and in the ways in which they express the timing of it relative to Easter and the resurrection of Christ. However, they are at one in naming it as a real experience that galvanised those who were present and after which none of them was the same again.

This elaboration of the role of the Spirit in the earliest community puts our thoughts about that community, whether then or now, into a theological framework. What they saw as bringing about this overall unity was the presence of the Holy Spirit dwelling among them and dwelling within them. Before anything else, these Christians were deeply conscious that they were 'baptised', as they put it, into the same fate and the same glory as Jesus Christ was.[5]

Moreover, they were a new body on the earth, a corporate Christ in some sense, and each one of them played some essential part in that body. It was similar to the way that any part of a human body, no matter how insignificant it may appear to be, has a role to play in the overall life and health of a person. With analogies like this, they conceived themselves as being one with Christ already: he was the head and they made up the parts of his body.

In the first letter of Peter we get the image from the Old

4. Acts 10:39-43.
5. See Rom 6:3-5.

Testament of the corner stone that has been rejected by the builders yet chosen by God.[6] This image is applied to Jesus, and his disciples are invited to group themselves around this stone as living stones in God's new temple: 'But you are a chosen race, a royal priesthood, a consecrated nation, a people set apart to sing the praises of God who called you out of the darkness into his wonderful light'.[7] The analogy of the body that is given by Paul in his first letter to the Corinthians is perhaps the best known of these imaginative constructs or pictures that are to be found in the early communities: 'Now you together are Christ's body; but each of you is a different part of it.'[8] In John we find similar ideas in his account of the last supper: 'As a branch cannot bear fruit all by itself, but must remain part of the vine, neither can you unless you remain in me. I am the vine, you are the branches.'[9]

These examples come from the earliest memories of the Christian community. We find in that community a people deeply conscious of itself as chosen by God and founded by him. That foundation is anchored in the special memory of the coming upon them of the spirit of Christ, the Holy One that anointed them with his courage and with his strength. It is from this tiny but expanding community that the gospel, which means literally 'the good news', of Christ's death and resurrection is spread. Communities and nations are forged in great or significant moments of history, frequently marked by victorious battles or successful revolutions. The Christian community was forged in the coming of the Holy Spirit upon the apostles and the disciples of Christ, a moment captured most graphically by the pen of Luke in his Acts of the Apostles.[10]

In his prayer for unity spoken at the last supper, Jesus asked: *I pray not only for these, but for those also who through their words*

6. See Ps 118:22 & par.
7. See 1 Pet 2:4-10; and Ex 19:3-8 & par, on which Peter's prophecy is based.
8. See 1 Cor 12:12-30.
9. See Jn 15:1-7.
10. Acts 2:1-13.

will believe in me. May they all be one. Father, may they be one in
us, as you are in me and I am in you, so that the world may believe
it was you who sent me.[11]

We should note the sense of 'not yet' and 'already' in the words of this prayer. Indeed, it may be one of the most unifying aspects of the community that it continually prays and intends these very words. Jesus did not assume that his disciples were already completely one. He asked his Father that *'they may be one'.*[12]

Community and celebration

One of the problems with any human insight, including religious insight, is that of sustaining it over a period of extended time. We are not talking here of ideas simply, or of practical matters which can be checked like the names in a telephone directory. We are talking about special insights that are real gifts.

People who are in love will know instinctively the nature of this problem: 'How do we keep our love for each other alive over the period of a lifetime?' In the context of religion, the question is: how is the faith, the interest and devotion of believers sustained indefinitely? Or, how can the bonding that takes place between the creature and the creator be maintained over the years and the generations, often through thick and thin? In the case of the Christian community, we are looking at a real bonding that is already present locally throughout the world, and that traces its origins to events that occurred, as we have seen, more than two thousand years ago.

This sustaining of God's gift, keeping it alive in the minds and hearts of men and women, is one reason for the existence of the church. As believing people, we need to belong together in some way so that our worshipping of God is shared with one another. We need to belong together to experience something of the love of God for us in the love that we bear to and receive

11. Jn 17:20-21.
12. These simple ideas are beautifully developed in Denys Turner's *Faith Seeking*, SCM Press, London, 2002, chapters 7 & 8, pp 66-74.

from one another. Our primary experience of this love of God takes place in the celebration of the eucharist.

Celebration marks the existence of a real community as nothing else does. While the celebration of sacrifices were universally thought of as ways of giving thanks to God in pre-Christian times, the eucharist replaces for Christians all the blood sacrifices of the old world, or the Old Covenant. The root meaning of the word eucharist is 'thanksgiving'.[13] The eucharist is our way of saying thanks to God. The words that are used today, 'he took bread and gave you thanks ... this is my body ... he took the cup, again he gave you thanks and praise ... this is the cup of my blood, the blood of the new and everlasting covenant ...'[14] are the very words that were used by Christ at the last supper.

The eucharist is an action and it is a entity. As an action, it is a gesture of sacrifice to God and one of self-giving by God to men and women. Each of these features is present in the celebration of the eucharist every day in our churches and in our communities. As an entity, the bread and the wine are the actual body and blood of Christ. Apart from a theological explanation which helps us to distinguish between the 'substance' of the bread and the 'accident', that is, the appearance of the bread, we do not actually know how this is the case. For St Thomas Aquinas, the eucharist is Jesus' greatest miracle.[15] It contains and presents God to us as something we can see and handle in our own hands and eat and drink with our mouths. In the eucharist, we have the truly wonderful reality, *res mirabilis*, literally, wonderful thing, given to us for our consumption and for our contemplation.

The eucharist, appearing to be bread and wine, while in reality being the body and blood of Christ, is both a symbol and at the same time what is symbolised. It offers us a template of what is going on throughout the community and throughout revel-

---

13. From the time of the prophet Hosea, c. 740 BC, the idea of 'thanksgiving' slowly began to eclipse the idea of 'blood sacrifice' in the theology of Israel. See Hosea 6:6 & par.
14. Mt 26:26-28 & par.
15. Opusc. 57. 4. Quoted in *The Divine Office*, Feast of Corpus Christi.

ation and the created world. We are living within the miraculous. God is everywhere; grace is everywhere.

The meaning of Church

The name for the believing community in which the writings of the New Testament were to emerge is *ekklesia*. This word is used in both the Greek version of the Old Testament and in the New Testament to translate the assembly of God's people. In the Old Testament, the *ekklesia* is the object of God's constancy and love. It is the focus of God's covenant with his people, and it symbolises also the unfaithful people that falls away from God and is called back to him. In the New Testament, the *ekklesia* is the successor to the former assembly of Israel. In New Testament times, as we have seen, the *ekklesia* can also be a source of scandal to Christians and to others, even though it is loved by God and redeemed by Christ. The common English translation of *ekklesia* is the word 'church'.

When we say that Jesus founded a church, 'upon this rock I will build my church',[16] we mean that a cell was put in place by him whereby the church that we know today has developed to its present form. That form has both an essential and a non-essential dimension. Much of the contemporary reflection concerning the institution of the church reflects on non-essential aspects of the Christian community, aspects that are conditioned, inevitably, by history and by culture. We can say, with confidence, that Jesus meant to inaugurate a celebrating community, and that he meant it to be marked in some form by his authority. The words 'upon this rock' are words that clearly applied to the apostle Peter,[17] who was nicknamed 'the Rock'. Like the first Peter, the church today is a human institution but, as founded by Christ, it is also divine.

---

16. Mt 16:18; see also Mt 10:1-4ff & par, on the calling and sending out of 'the twelve'. The term 'apostles' clearly came to include also Paul, although he was not one of the twelve, nor did he accompany the Saviour during his lifetime here on earth.

17. The Greek *'epi taute te Petra'* means 'on this rock'; Peter is *'Petros'*.

Part of the difficulty of loving the church is a tendency to think of it institutionally. We must broaden our horizons. If we think of the baptismal font to which each of us was brought, a more sympathetic context may emerge. The baptismal font provides a vision of the nucleus of a shared journey of faith. The maternal and the paternal influences that may have had a beneficial influence in our lives can be discerned in that familial group. It is in that group, and its pastor, that we learn to recognise the reality of church. This is the group that is first and foremost the believing community. We get a strong sense of this in the writings of Justin Martyr who lived in the second century AD.

On Sundays there is an assembly of all who live in towns or in the country, and the memoirs of the apostles or the writings of the prophets are read for as long as time allows.

Then the reading is brought to an end, and the president delivers an address in which he admonishes and encourages us to imitate in our own lives the beautiful lessons we have heard read.

Then we all stand up together and pray. When we have finished the prayer, as I have said, bread and wine and water are brought up; the president offers prayers and thanksgiving as best he can, and the people say 'Amen' as an expression of their agreement. Then follows the distribution of the food over which the prayer of thanksgiving has been recited; all present receive some of it, and the deacons carry some to those who are absent.

Those who are well provided for, if they wish to do so, contribute what each thinks fit; this is collected and left with the president, so that he can help the orphans and the widows and the sick, and all who are in need for any other reason, such as prisoners and visitors from abroad; in short he provides for all who are in want.[18]

In a contemporary setting, this local atmosphere comes across clearly in Paula's thinking. I had asked her about her participation in her local parish:

18 This excerpt comes from chap 67 of Justin's 'Apology in defence of the Christians'. For 'The President' read priest or bishop. Quoted in *The Divine Office*, II, Eastertide, Week 3 Sunday. On Baptism, see Justin, idem, chap 61. Quoted in *The Divine Office*, II, Eastertide week 3, Wednesday.

I do the church collection ... I go to Mass every Sunday ... I mean it's a great old parish ... I was only saying to Fr John the other day ... it was great because you got to meet all the people going to Mass, because it (the temporary parish church) *was so small ... and he was saying that he hopes that when the new church is built that I'll feel the same way ...*

The impression of the importance of the local focus comes across very strongly when she discusses the priest:

If he weren't there, who would be there to keep us going, and to keep the faith going and all the rest? How can I put this, I always like to put it in layman's terms ... he works for God, right ... he has to answer to the bishop ... he's somewhere down the line ... but ... he would be the one to keep the faith in the parish. I mean if we hadn't got him we'd have no church to go to ... a priest has a very big part ... he keeps things ticking over, you know ... that's the way I feel. I mean he would be the one that the parish would go to first if there is anything wrong ... he's the first person we all approach ... yes ... I have the height of respect for the priest.

Yet it emerges from my conversation with Martin that the local clergy do not always provide the leadership that Paula has experienced:

Because I see so many people who I think are automatons, and merely mouthing ... because it is funny how people spot it ... I occasionally go to Mass with my daughter-in-law and sometimes she will say 'He's not a very good priest.' And I will say 'Why?' And she will say 'Did you notice how he said Mass? He doesn't mean a word of it, it doesn't mean anything to him.' And in my heart of hearts I would have to admit she's right too. And it is sad that it should be so, and its sad for the individual that he has reached a point where the words do not mean anything to him, the ceremony doesn't mean anything to him anymore.

I would love to have been able at times to replace the man on the altar, and say to him: 'For God's sake, will you talk about things that really matter to the audience, about their everyday lives, things that affect their everyday lives.' At the same time, I recognise that,

to continue to do that, sermon after sermon after sermon, Sunday
after Sunday after Sunday, and when you have a captive audience
... capable of leading them, or influencing them or whatever you
like, that the motivation, the spark, would become quite low at times
... and you would have difficulties ...

Part of the function of the Christian community, as we have
seen, is the provision of ceremony; that is the naming of the unseen and the conducting of dialogue with the invisible world.
But ceremony, being a celebration of the invisible, should always be on its guard to tell the truth. Ceremony can too easily
become a delusion and a lie. Similarly, ceremony or speech that
lacks conviction and sincerity, or speech that comes more from
an ideology rather than from the love of God and other people,
is more likely to promote scandal in its hearers than lead them to
devotion.

Political power and the Church
Discussion of the church as being human inevitably brings to
mind the perspective of political power and the institution. The
whole reality of power, and its associated realities of favour,
privilege, sanctions and force, is the focus of intense study in
modern and post-modern culture. Institutions of every kind are
analysed by observers and critics from this point of view.
Observers point out the limits and the shortcomings of the exercise of power and they reflect on the abuses of power that are
engendered in institutions and by them. This is part of the context
in which power in the church must also be understood in our
time. The human sciences provide us with important insights
about this human element. The role of such sciences in understanding the church has not always been clearly recognised by
Christians in the past.

Power may be defined as the ability to do or act, whether as
an individual or as a body or as an authority. There is no short-
age of passages in the gospels outlining the teaching of Jesus on
this subject, even to the point of contrasting his disciples' use of
power with how power is handled in the wider civil community.

Perhaps Jesus epitomised his views by washing the feet of the apostles at the last supper.[19] His disciples were to be the servants of all. The issue of power is thus of particular importance for Christians. If we think back to the last supper, however, we can see Jesus waiting with basin and towel for many who confidently, but ignorantly, practise in his name.

Sociology interrogates human relationships on the basis of the power that may be supposed to be inherently operating within them. By its very method as a science, sociology suspends belief in all ultimate questions so as to focus on what are called the 'power' questions that may need to be answered first. In studying the church, for example, it removes God and the unseen world completely from the frame. It invites us to focus only on the interactions themselves that take place between us as a consequence of the beliefs we hold, particularly those interactions that are related to power and to its privileges.

However, when states or banks, for example, are criticised for their usages of power, people are not tempted to forget that either politics or money is important. In the case of religion, however, it is possible to forget God and that to which religion ultimately refers, and to think of everything only in terms of what goes on here on earth. We can forget to piece together again the whole picture which had been disassembled simply to make an important point. In putting back the wider picture, we must introduce the lessons that have been learned.

Used positively, power is an opportunity to bring about good. Used negatively, power can be totally destructive. The difficulties encountered here are those associated with what is called purity of heart. Christians, including the most dedicated, are tempted to emphasise their own vision of the truth at the expense of the vision of others. It can seem that openness equates with weakness which clearly it does not.

Scandal and the Church
Travelling back in time several centuries, it is clear that the

19. Jn 13:3-17.

Inquisition represents a period of shame in the history of the church. It was the inquisition that persecuted and martyred people that it suspected were of doubtful faith. It has been difficult to imagine a greater counter sign to that of Jesus Christ than this. In a very real sense, the inquisition was the complete moral failure of the church at the end of the Middle Ages. It is understandable that church leaders should now seek to apologise for that failure. Over the last five hundred years and more, the inquisition has provided not only Catholics but also all people of good will with sufficient reason to be severely scandalised by the church.

Yet we have to remember that Jesus warned his disciples that scandals would come. Speaking of the innocence of children he said:

Anyone who welcomes a little child like this in my name welcomes me. But anyone who is an obstacle to bring down one of these little ones who have faith in me would be better drowned in the depths of the sea with a great millstone around his neck. Alas for the world that there should be such obstacles! Obstacles indeed there must be, but alas for the one who provides them![20]

Catholics in recent times are particularly sensitive to and ashamed of the scandals that dominate news of the church. The situation is particularly acute in the Irish church and in churches that have spread out from Irish roots in the English-speaking world. This scandal focuses on child sex abuse carried out continuously by some members of the clergy and by some religious. This abuse was covered up and not acknowledged by their superiors. It is a scandal that has caused, and continues to cause, incalculable pain to individuals who were abused and to parents who had expected protection for their children in the shelter of the parish or the Catholic school.

No small part in this scandal was played by the culture of silence that refused to listen to what abused children themselves had to say. The abused child had nowhere to go.[21]

20. Mt 18:5-7.
21. See Richard Webster, *Why Freud Was Wrong*, London 1995, pp 511-

One might say that it was only a minority of clergy that were involved in child sexual abuse. But this is a totally inadequate statement of what happened. Wrong acts will, of course, happen, and we ought not be blind to this. But the fear of facing those acts because of possible scandal, or in order to maintain power and image at the expense of truth, can never be justified. Shamed by association, Catholics know that what happened should never have been tolerated in its happening.

Yet as we turn into this new century, we enter also upon a time of hope for the church. Some see the very scarcity of vocations to the priesthood and religious life in our cultures as a sign of hope. No one could ever say that the absence of a wise priest was in any sense a blessing, yet it may well be that the absence of 'too many' priests is a blessing. It may be that the Christian community is about to undergo profound changes for the good in the years ahead, and that a re-balancing of the roles of the clergy and the laity in the community, and in responsibility for the community, is part of that movement of change.

Difficulties at this time

A strong sense of the difficulty of 'holding on' in the modern church emerged from three of my conversations. Paula, Martin and Suzanne each referred to a crisis. It is impossible to treat of the Christian faith in any thorough way at this time without addressing what people see as critical difficulties. Some questions

---

528. One looks in vain for a full account of the damage of sexual abuse on the child victim in Masters, Johnson and Kolodny, *Human Sexuality*, New York, 1992. This was the fourth edition of the main text from a liberal and secular background available to teachers and the public generally on the subject of sexuality for many years. In the section 'Behaviour Patterns of Child Molesters', pp 427-430 they do refer the reader to the work of Finkelhor, *Child Sexual Abuse*, New York, 1984; in this book an alarm is sounded to the real danger encountered by children in child abuse. Similarly, a treatment of the damage of child abuse does not appear in John Money, *Lovemaps*, New York, 1986. Money was then the main theorist of paedophilia and of the so called 'Philias'. He is more concerned in his work to counter what he sees as the 'anti-sexual' thought of the puritanical strain in North American culture. See pp 153-161, 'Victimology'.

persist in the minds of the faithful, even when the teaching authority of the church would seem to have attempted to bring speculation on such issues to closure. On other matters, difficulties continue to persist even when the authority of the church has recognised a need for some flexibility.

Among the issues where closure has been stated are: the use of all forms of contraception in marriage; the participation of women in the ministerial priesthood and the authoritative structures of the church; the issue of marriage for clergy in the western rite; the practice of general absolution on certain ordinary occasions. Other matters on which some flexibility has been shown include the possible readmission to Holy Communion of some who have been divorced and remarried without the benefit of a church annulment; whether one can ever vote in favour of abortion legislation or support counselling strategies that may include the giving of some information regarding the availability of abortion; or whether a negative understanding of homosexuality is appropriate. All of these issues came up in one or other of the three conversations I have mentioned without any prompting on my part.

Many Catholics who have sincere doubts about any of these issues named above continue in their practice and loyalty to their faith, and feel bound, to a greater or lesser extent by a spirit of obedience. They believe that, at some later time, these issues will come to be resolved in the believing community in some better manner than they are now.[22] On the other hand, many Catholics appear to have quietly withdrawn from their practice within the believing community because they disagree with some or any of these issues.

These questions constitute a kind of 'fault line' that runs across the credibility of the church today. It is not as if there is total disagreement on the whole question of contraception, nor indeed on many issues confronting heterosexuality as well as homosexuality, nor indeed on the status of church annulments, nor on the other issues that I have mentioned. Yet, people on ei-

22. Newman's account of the development of doctrine and the clash of

ther side of the line, no matter how sincere in their faith, can find it difficult to communicate openly with those who are on the other side. There can be a kind of mirror imaging that takes place among those who man the opposite sides of a divide, a co-dependence even, whereby people on opposite sides define themselves by their very opposition to each other. It may be that the way forward lies, for the moment, not so much in the further resolution of any of these issues but in a deeper issue that under-cuts them. That deeper issue is the greater participation of ordi-nary Catholics in the thinking through of doctrinal issues, espe-cially issues that concern them particularly.

The coming of such a spirit of change was one of the signals that emerged from the Second Vatican Council. The Council spoke very insistently on a new role for the laity and, by implication, for the clergy. It spoke in a new way of the whole community, not so much as hierarchy and faithful but as the 'People of God'.[23]

It is important, also, to remember that many of the 'archi-tects' of the Second Vatican Council had been 'silenced' by an oppressive church style that had dominated Catholicism. They were surprised to find themselves thrust forward in the Council, and their views heard willingly at last.[24] In fact, it is important to recall how different in complexion and flexibility the answer to

opposing ideas allows him to defend a view of church authority that has elements that can appear harsh and peremptory. Controversialists may have their hands tied. He emphasises the timeliness of things. See *Letters and Diaries*, op. cit., xix, pp 179-80. In his own day the conflict be-tween religious and secular knowledge was causing great confusion among believers: *'at the moment it is so difficult to say precisely what it is that is to be encountered and overthrown ... hypotheses rise and fall.'* Newman here obeys the restrictive teachings of Pius IX on questions of science. He concludes: *'And so far from finding a difficulty in obeying in this case, I have cause to be thankful and to rejoice to have so clear a direction in a matter of difficulty.'* *Apologia pro Vita Sua*, op. cit., (chap 5). See Ker's mas-terly commentary on this chapter of the *Apologia* in *John Henry Newman*, op. cit., pp 548-559.

23. See *The Documents of Vatican II*, op. cit., Constitution on the Church, chaps.2, 4,

24. One hundred years previously this had been the experience of Newman as a Catholic. His view of the role of the laity in the church

the question 'What is the church?' became between the short span of years when the Council began and when it had ended. When we take the longer view, it is important to recognise that there are or may be truths or aspects of the truth 'whose time has not yet come.'[25]

A petition in the *The Divine Office* captures perfectly the prayer for today and for the future of the believing community:

> *May the whole church be guided by your Holy Spirit; let all who call themselves Christians be led into the way of truth and hold the faith in unity of spirit.*[26]

was considered as almost heretical at that time; see Gilley, op. cit. pp 312ff. His acceptance of the sober restraint of an English piety was rejected by many, including some of his fellow converts from Anglicanism, who embraced an overwrought Italianate piety in life and in doctrinal attitudes; see Gilley, op. cit. pp 350ff.

25. When he was at work on his *On Consulting the Faithful in Matters of Doctrine*, Newman wrote: '*I did all I could to ascertain God's will, and that being the case, I am sure good will come of my taking it – I am of opinion that the Bishops see only one side of things, and I have a mission, as far as my own internal feelings go, against evils which I see. On the other hand, I have always preached that things which are really useful, still are done, according to God's will, at one time, not at another – and that if you attempt at a wrong time, what is in itself right, you perhaps become a heretic or a schismatic. What I may aim at may be real and good, but it may be God's will it should be done a hundred years later ... When I am gone, it will be seen perhaps that persons stopped me from doing a work which I might have done. God overrules all things. Of course it is discouraging to be out of joint with the time, and to be snubbed and stopped as soon as I begin to act.*' *Letters and Diaries*, C. S. Dessain (ed.), Oxford, 1961ff, xix, 179, and quoted in Selby, op. cit., p 33, and Ker, op. cit. p 553.

26. Evening Prayer, Week 4, Wednesday.

CHAPTER TWELVE

The God I Believe in and why

For the last eleven chapters of this book, I have sought to set out my reasons for believing in God. The irony is that the God that I believe in cannot, in one sense, be known at all. I don't believe that we can have, on our own initiative, any direct knowledge of God. Although I may attempt to scrutinise the smallness of the atom or the greatness of the stars that comprise the universe, I find that this scrutiny is not much help when it comes to issues of God. I find that there is only a kind of evidence that may point to causes, or that may not. I am left with questions rather than answers. And, initially at any rate, I find myself with choices rather than certainty.

There is not only a question about whether or not a God exists. There is equally a question about a God that I may suppose to exist as opposed to a God that anybody else might suppose to exist. There can only be one God. A God that is unjust or one that is without mercy is not the God that I believe in. I cannot have faith in a God that I do not believe in. The God that may exist has to be the God that I believe in or else my whole argument collapses.

When I reflect on my own existence, I find myself in the territory of God. That is, when I reflect on the fact that I am, and when I reflect on who it is that I am, such reflections lead inevitably to the question of how these facts came to be. What is their significance, if any? This shifts quickly to the issue of mortality; to a time when I will be dead; and what does this hold for me, if anything? Will this time be for me a nothing? Or will it be a time that is rich in meaning? Growing up, these were my questions.

While they were questions about myself, they pointed always beyond me. They highlighted that further and more ultimate question, the question of God. In other words, to be perplexed with the question of oneself led me inexorably to the question of God. It has always seemed to me that the question of God was of the utmost importance. This religious legacy was a significant aspect of what education had done for me.

Why was I then willing to believe in God? How is it that I believe when so many of my contemporaries do not? Is there something I see that they do not see? Or, as they might put it, am I being fooled by something that is not really there? Am I deceived by the wish to believe, by my own naïvety or need, rather than viewing the facts as they are?

Some personal reasons for my belief

To me, belief is born of a trust of underlying reality. It may sound deceptively simple but, basically, that is how it is. I trust reality in all that it is. In an age that is willing to subscribe to the idea of the 'unconscious', this ought not be too difficult an undertaking. I am not sure what indeed underlying reality is, but then who is? For me, belief in underlying reality is very simply a belief in something like the providence of God, a providence that, in the last analysis, envisages the good of each person.

It may happen that I do not feel any sense of God at all; at times, for example, there is no overarching sense of security or wonder. I experience moods of uncertainty, difficulty and even doubt. And yet, in and through all of this, somehow I have a basic trust: I was born, I live, I will be happy, I will suffer, I will die. Through it all, there is some ultimate meaning, even if now I cannot see what that meaning is.

The trust I experience is like the trust that comes to exist between two people who love each other deeply. Partners in a marriage that has endured for thirty or forty years may well look at each other and say: 'How is it that we know and trust each other?' They trust because they have learned to trust, they have learned what trust is. They have come to depend and to rely on each other in a particular way. They distinguish between the substance of what goes on between them and the accidents; misunderstandings between them are unlikely to be permanent. Trusting deep down in reality is something like this.

Implicit in this trusting of reality there is the willingness to worship. I find myself willing to bow down to all that is, to accept reality. This acceptance is part of my being. I experience it in a thousand positive contexts: an ocean wave, a starry night, the gaze of a child. And it is there in the negative contexts also: a wave that destroys a city points towards the utterly 'other' agenda that is present in the upheavals taking place on the ocean floor. For me, it is an acceptance that looks beyond the immediate context in which it occurs. It says 'yes' to God, even to a God that appears to be indifferent or helpless in the face of earthly disasters. It says 'yes' to God as a complete mystery.

When contemplating or bowing down before everything, or the 'everything' that is apparent to me, I identify an eternal significance in things. In other words, I see something that goes well beyond the ordinary, the every day. Part of this awareness is a sense of my own uniqueness and that of every other person. My uniqueness is tied in with that sense I have that there is only one 'me'. Only one person can exist in my shoes. At the level of who we are, none of us is interchangeable. I am convinced of this. This uniqueness begins with our genes but ends in each one of us being a separate and distinct individual human being. I have a strong sense of my own uniqueness and, in this, I believe that I am not deceived. Unique I am, and this uniqueness, I further believe, has its origins in one who is the source of all distinctiveness.

Something about the history of my belief may be helpful here. When I was young, I had some knowledge about myself from experience: I knew that I was and I knew something of who I was. But of God, I had only 'taught and learned' knowledge, an important but a very different kind of knowing. I had no personal experience to back up this knowledge.

The kind of God that I believed in during my formative years was a benign God. That God was never harsh or indifferent to people and to how they felt. Somehow the 'harsh' God passed me by. Sermons that I listened to with a harsh message invariably provoked confusion and anger, and compliance with their spirit was short-lived. To what extent this was due to parental influences or to the example of my teachers, I cannot say. Many people who grew up with me, and many who came after me, clearly had a different experience.

The crisis that often hits people in their teens or early twenties became very real for me. It began to happen, quite suddenly, that all I had been taught about God started to fall away. Initially, there was something very frightening about this situation. I had no longer any notion that 'he' actually existed or that 'he' could exist. Coming to terms with this aspect of reality was something very new and challenging. Yet, if there was no God, I had to face it.

There followed long periods that were characterised by a sense of God's absence rather than his presence. These were cold and lonely years. In those years, I lived spiritually from hand to mouth, seeking eagerly and not finding very much. It was in those lean years that I learned to trust in what sustained others and yet did nothing for me. This ranged from attraction to the lives of particular saints to a blind participation in the eucharist, even without any sense of the rightness of what I was doing.

And then that searching came to an end. I made a decision to believe in God rather than in no God. This was a choice on my part.

To make an act of faith is to exercise a kind of choice. In my experience, faith does not drop unannounced on the unsuspecting soul. The person chooses to believe. This choice can be based on any number of reasons in different cases. In my own case, the possibility of there being nothing to explain was just too overwhelming to be true. It was overwhelming, not simply in the initial impact of such an idea but, also, in the long term, in the lasting impression that such an idea creates. It was overwhelming in what one was left with: nothing at all. I cannot believe in an explanation of the universe that excludes the idea of God. Such a view, for me, comes down, ultimately, to nothing.

What I found then was simply peace, a sense of resting in something that was not me, something that was vast. This was my re-entry into a sense of God. This sense of God has been with me ever since. I dread a day when it may be withdrawn again. After thirty years such an eventuality would be a real shock to the system. But if that day should come, I pray that I will be, with God's help, equal to it.

A God who has already spoken to us

There is another context within which I find ways of knowing God, namely through 'Revelation'. Abroad on the mainstream of culture is the amazing claim that the hidden God has spoken already to men and to women. Today, it is possible to forget or to overlook entirely, the supposed fact that God has addressed himself to humanity. This communication is at the heart of my belief and sustains me in it.

To the reader of this book, it will be evident that my faith rests on God's revelation. It is not my intention here to go over again what has already been said. I have chosen, rather, two pieces from the scripture that point up, for me, the wholesomeness of religious faith. The first is simply the following affirmation:

> *How gracious is the Lord, and just;*
> *Our God has compassion.*[1]

I think that these words convey the essential quality of God. It seems that I know this because I know that graciousness, justice and compassion are at the heart of the good human being. In other words, I respond to God with an understanding of what it is to be human.

Graciousness is that complete kindness of which some people are capable. Justice is a strength, a moral composure, that assures that there will be no let down, no weakness, in the face

---

1. Ps 114 (116.5).

of duplicity. Compassion is a quality of mercy that balances strength in the soul. People who are conscientious and wise in their quest for God acquire a balance of these qualities. Such people, be they light-hearted or be they weighed down with the experience of the world, and often they are both of these, remind us of the reality of God.

The second quotation is as follows:

We teach what scripture calls: the things that no eye has seen and no ear has heard, things beyond the mind of man, all that God has prepared for those who love him.[2]

Somehow my late father had made these words his own. He may have learned them at his mother's knee or, perhaps, from a teacher when he went to school. They were the only words of scripture that I ever heard on his lips, and when he spoke them he did so with a kind of intonation that brooked no opposition! Nobody would describe my Dad as a pious man; yet he was dutiful and felt bound by the commandments of God. The words come from St Paul's First letter to the Corinthians, a matter of detail that he is unlikely to have known. These words express for me an underlying confidence in the goodness of God, and a sense that God has some kind of providence that is preparing everything for the good. As with my Dad's intonation, it always seemed that God's good purpose would prevail, whatever tragedies or disasters might accompany them.

A God of mercy was revealed in Jesus Christ. Time and time again, whether in parables or in his quotations from the Old Testament, or in his personal actions, Jesus speaks of the mercy of God. 'What I want is mercy, not sacrifice …'[3] seems to be written on every page of the gospels. This was fully in line with the God that I thought was credible. Even when Jesus was harsh, and he was exceedingly harsh towards the religious leaders of his own day, 'you white-washed tombs …'[4] he called them, this harshness was but the negative side of his feelings of love and

---

2. 1 Cor 2:9-10a.
3. Mt 9:12-13; Hos 6.
4. Mt 23:27-28

kindness for the people. He is frustrated by the hypocrisy of his would-be shepherds. Even where he appears to be 'against' what is bad, we find that God is always 'for' what is good.

In Jesus we have, I believe, the authentic stamp of God. Jesus belongs to the realm of faith. Faith is, of course, the nub of this book.

The reality of faith

Faith is a 'looking beyond' nature and fact to another kind of reality. It is about that which I cannot see. It is pitched in a totally different arena, yet it is one that is familiar to me.

The different arena of faith is like that of anticipation, an anticipation that is often borne out in everyday experience. To anticipate is to look forward to something that is not present now. We readily anticipate a holiday, or a wedding, or a birth, or death. Faith is an anticipation that God exists and that he has prepared a home for us when we die. Yet it is more than this: faith is a taking on trust of the present existence of God, a taking on trust of the eternal existence of God 'who was, is now and ever shall be'.

Faith is open to reason, and need not be closed to it. It is always reasonable to believe the Christian revelation, even if the holding of that belief is also something that is beyond reason. It is entirely possible that something can be in excess of reason but not in any way contradictory to it. So it is with Christian faith.

I believe that God is the great mystery that binds the universe together. He has to be the ultimate unifying factor. At the natural level, it is altogether to be expected that I have almost no notion of what 'he' may be like. Inevitably I tend to think of 'him' in human terms, in images that are bound by time and space. But God is beyond all of our categories. That 'he' is something actual and that 'he' exists seems to be about as far as I can go. But the God that I believe in has not left us in ignorance; he has given us 'his' son. In a sense everything is complete: we have in Jesus a grounding of the mystery of God. 'This is my son. Follow him.'[5]

5. Baptism of Jesus, Mt 3:13-17 & par.; Transfiguration of Jesus, Mt 17.1-8 & par.

A God that is present to my deepest moments, whether of joy or of despair, is the God that I believe in. To choose to believe in such a God as this, to give one's heart and mind to the truth of such a belief, is what faith means to me. And it is here precisely that I have found what can only be called a reciprocation of my belief. My belief is somehow sustained by divine grace once the choice was made. I had to decide, make up my own mind, as freely as I could, to believe in God. This freedom was to play an important part in all that followed. But on my deciding to say 'yes', many of my difficulties disappeared.

Overall my decision has given me a sense of wellbeing, or religious consolation. It is a consolation that can be, and that has been, shaken by many of life's tragedies, whether at home or at a distance. And it can be shaken by the reality of injustice. Yet it is a wellbeing that re-asserts itself, it returns to its equilibrium eventually. It is ultimately confident because it knows its own peace and whence this peace is derived. In this confidence, I found myself living and enjoying the life that I had been attracted to as a young man. As could be with any life, this was despite the problems and frustrations that came with it.

So, I find that I can make the sign of the cross. I believe in the Father, in the Son, and in the Holy Spirit. That there are three manifestations of God, I accept. That there is one God, I accept. I do not question what I have no prospect of understanding. It is there simply.

I find, moreover, that I can accept God's gift of faith as an essential dimension of my life on earth. This makes it possible for me to believe that the universe, the world and life have been given. If these have all been given, what is there to prevent me from believing that more will be given? What prevents me from believing in an entry into eternity and mystery that will last forever and that will be the fulfilment of my deepest desires? Nothing does.